STUDIES IN GERMAN LITERATURE

Volume XVIII

□ □

HANS FALLADA

HUMANIST AND SOCIAL CRITIC

by

H. J. SCHUELER

York University,
Canada

1970

MOUTON

THE HAGUE · PARIS

Printed in The Netherlands by Mouton & Co., Printers, The Hague.

TO
MY MOTHER
AND
TO THE MEMORY OF
MY FATHER

PREFACE

In most books dealing with German literature, the name of Hans Fallada (Rudolf Ditzen, 1893–1947) is either conspicuous by its absence or only mentioned in passing as that of a „minor" author whose works merit only the most perfunctory consideration. This situation illustrates once again the fact that the rather meaningless division, which has so often been made in the past in German literary discussion, between *Dichtung* and *Literatur*, involves the inevitable exclusion from any serious study of the works of those authors believed to belong to the latter and what is, needless to say, felt to be the inferior category. The whole phenomenon seems to be a curious and lamentable outcropping of the highbrow dogma of German *Bildung* which is only gradually being overcome. Hans Fallada himself, incidentally, always insisted, with a sense of rebellious pride, that he was not a *Dichter* but „only" a *Schriftsteller*. In the essay entitled „Wie ich Schriftsteller wurde", contained in the recently published *Gesammelte Erzählungen* (1967), Fallada even goes so far as to refer to himself simply as a „Bücherschreiber".

In Fallada's case we are faced with a special paradox; for the disregard of his work by German literary scholars, and the judgment it implies, stands in reverse relationship to the opinion of the international reading public. Fallada's remarkable, worldwide popularity stands in a rather absurd contrast to his almost complete neglect by the critics and historians of German literature. Furthermore, those few but competent opinions that have occasionally been voiced on Fallada by a number of ardent students of his work as well as by some personal friends, show

clearly how erroneous and unfortunate such a neglect is; for
they are almost unanimous in their praise of Fallada's great
epic talent even though it may be argued that they overshoot
their mark somewhat when, in some cases, they name our author
in one breath with such figures as Grimmelshausen, Zola, Balzac
and Hauptmann. It is an encouraging sign, at any rate, that Hans
Fallada has recently joined the train of illustrious literary personalities which makes up Rowohlt's series „rororo Bild Mono-
graphien". Jürgen Manthey's interesting and well-written little
biography of Hans Fallada, which appeared in this series in 1963,
represents an important step forward on the road to establishing
Fallada as an author deserving the serious attention of literary
scholars. Manthey's work does not, however, purport to be
anything more than a biography. His main concern, Manthey
states, is to give „einen Lebensbericht und keine Werkbeschreibung".[1] No critical „Werkbeschreibung" that does proper justice
to Hans Fallada has as yet been written. It is the main purpose
of this study to attempt to fill the gap created by the continuing
lack of such an inquiry.

Hans Fallada entered the German literary scene in a period of
extreme social, economic and political dislocation. It was a time
when the general disillusionment and disintegration had reached
a degree of such intensity that, to many German writers, only an
attitude of complete objective detachment seemed to hold out a
promise of coping plausibly with the problems of the day. The
term *die neue Sachlichkeit* indicates this change in perspective.
Hans Fallada is usually classified as a representative of this trend
in modern German fiction which succeeded the intricate and often
morbid introspections of the post-World War I psychological
novelists. While it is quite misleading to pigeonhole Fallada in this
manner, it is nevertheless true that he, too, surveyed German
social life, shattered by the aftermath of the First World War, in
a spirit of detached yet also deeply involved *Sachlichkeit*. Objective
narration is certainly one of the hallmarks of Fallada's greatest

---

[1] Jürgen Manthey, *Hans Fallada* (Reinbek bei Hamburg, Rowohlt Verlag,
1963), p. 106.

novels and his social criticism is, consequently, always devoid
of any political bias or partisan sentiments and constantly illumi-
nates his strong humanistic concerns. Contrary to widely held
views, Hans Fallada is not a political and social writer in the
generally accepted sense of those terms. Even in his first great
novel, *Bauern, Bonzen und Bomben* (1931), which is usually
classified as a „political novel" (Kurt Tucholsky called the book
„nur ein politisch hochinteressanter Roman"),[2] Fallada's constant
emphasis on the plight of the human being as such is already
clearly evident. It was to certain timeless and universal issues and
problems of man's social life, then, that Hans Fallada devoted his
main attention. And it is from this point of view that we propose
to discuss the social criticism of this dedicated humanist.

The following chapters are an attempt to discuss those issues
of man's social life with which Hans Fallada was predominantly
concerned. The first chapter discusses our author's interpretation
of the social and moral predicament of members of a social class
which in a very real sense „made" Hans Fallada: the German
Kleinbürgertum. Our second chapter elaborates further on the
theme of the *Kleinbürger*, this time viewing him within the context
of his private life. It investigates the theme of marriage and the
role of woman both in relation to the social life of the „little
man" and in its wider and more general social relevance. The
third and fourth chapters deal with Hans Fallada's presentation
of the problems of modern man's adjustment to society and life
in an age which is both highly industrialised and urbanised
(Chapter III) and essentially atomistic (Chapter IV). The fourth
chapter also attempts to shed some light on Fallada's views on
man's ultimate metaphysical gropings for basic spiritual values
beyond the artificial confines of the social world. In the brief
concluding chapter an attempt is made to form an estimate of
Fallada's achievements and of his position in German literature
of the twentieth century. A biography of Hans Fallada was not
included in this study, since this has already been provided by

² Kurt Tucholsky, *Gesammelte Werke* (Reinbek bei Hamburg, Rowohlt
Verlag, 1960), III, 822.

Jürgen Manthey as well as by Theodor Lemmer in his dissertation, entitled *Hans Fallada, Eine Monographie* (diss. Freiburg in der Schweiz, 1961). Lemmer has also given synopses of all of Fallada's major works as well as excerpts from his two early expressionist novels. Lemmer's extensive and valuable analysis of Fallada's style and of his narrative techniques obviated the need to discuss this subject in detail in our investigation.

For the author this study has been, in a very real sense, a labour of love. The task will have been richly rewarded if this contribution will help to bring our much neglected author closer to the minds and hearts of the students and admirers of what is most reassuring in German literature of this century.

York University   H. J. Schueler
Toronto, Canada

CONTENTS

Preface 7

I. The Plight of the „Kleinbürger" 13

II. Marriage and the Role of Woman 39

III. The Return to the Soil 64

IV. The Isolation of the Individual 87

V. Hans Fallada's Legacy 113

Selected Bibliography 120

I

THE PLIGHT OF THE „KLEINBÜRGER"

Whenever and wherever the name of Hans Fallada is mentioned the immediate comment is likely to take the form of a reference to the title of the novel which, deservedly, won the author international recognition and, in twenty different tongues, carried the image of the „little man" to the four corners of the earth: *Kleiner Mann – was nun?* (1932). Thus Hans Fallada's name and fame in German literature has been inextricably linked to the figure of the „little man" and rightly so. For it is as the avowed spokesman of members of that social class which occupies the lower section of the diversified social scale, which constitutes the German *Bürgertum*, that Hans Fallada deserves to hold a prominent and significant position in modern German literature, a position which still awaits his installation. If there have been acclaimed poets of all other social classes, Hans Fallada stands out as the author of the German *Kleinbürgertum*, and it is as such that we shall be concerned with him in this chapter. We shall see that it is the economically weak *Kleinbürger* and his desperate struggle for a livelihood in a highly competitive and capitalistic society, especially during periods of social and economic crises such as inflation and unemployment, that matters every time for Hans Fallada and provides the central theme of many of his best novels. We shall also see that Fallada has some interesting observations to make regarding the characteristics that are peculiar to the social status of his „little man".

It was in his great unemployment novel *Kleiner Mann – was nun?* that Hans Fallada not only for the first time explicitly named his pet but also, in the figure of Johannes Pinneberg, presented the very personification of the „little man" and gave a clear picture of some of the main problems confronting his social class. This novel was conceived and written while the author was himself without a source of income. The nightmare of unemployment with its concomitant ghost of poverty and the spectacle of an eerie dance of hordes of numbers symbolising the power of money as a lever of social prestige and economic power never really loosened its grip on Fallada's imagination. Recalling that distressing yet fateful and formative period of his career, Hans Fallada writes in one of his autobiographical books:

Das waren Zeiten! Das waren Stunden tiefster Bekümmernis! ... Wir hatten nichts – nur Sorgen und schlaflose Nächte! ... Der Schreck jener Zeit sitzt heute noch so fest in mir, daß ich jede Rechnung sofort am Tage ihres Eingangs bezahle.
ich hieß nur „Der arme Arbeitslose mit Kind".
. . . .
Was lag in einer solchen Situation näher, als ein Buch zu schreiben des Titels: „Kleiner Mann – was nun?" An den Nachmittagen und Abenden, in den bedrücktesten Tagen meines Lebens schrieb ich dies Buch. [1]

Hans Fallada's profound understanding of all the many and varied problems that arise out of unemployment and his deep sympathy with the predicament of the victims of adverse economic conditions give convincing evidence of a knowledge which is of the first-hand order.

In *Kleiner Mann – was nun?*, more than in any other of his tales of post-World War I demoralisation, Fallada recorded the atmosphere of complete disillusionment and hopelessness which engulfed millions of people during one of the most complicated periods of German economic and social history, a period that was witnessing the gradual dissolution of the Weimar Republic and the rising tide of National Socialism. Seldom has a writer presented such an accurate reflection of the state of mind engendered in the German people during this period of grave dislocations. It is in an atmosphere of utter despondency that the „little man",

---

[1] *Heute bei uns zu Haus* (Stuttgart and Berlin, Rowohlt Verlag, 1943), pp. 32-33.

Pinneberg, and his „Lämmchen" set out on the adventure of their marriage. Fallada's most popular novel can, of course, be primarily read as a love story describing this trying yet exciting and rewarding adventure of two young people. It is, indeed, more likely than not that the immense popularity of the book is due to a large extent to its appeal as a story of the trials and conquests of two lovers who become utterly disenchanted with everything but their almost Kleistian trust in each other. There is no reason why the book cannot and should not be read and appreciated in this manner. For *Kleiner Mann – was nun?* is doubtless one of the most moving love stories in modern literature – whatever its critics might say about the „sentimental" elements of the book. What the power of simple and trusting love can do to comfort and heal an anguished soul has seldom been portrayed more convincingly. In the end it is „das Beisammenseinkönnen" of two loving souls that remains as a bulwark against all demoralising forces of modern society. But clearly this was not all that Fallada wanted to depict in his novel. The book is also a very astute social study showing Fallada's intimate knowledge of the particular handicap with which the *Kleinbürger*, his „litle man", has to contend in his desperate attempt to secure a firm and viable basis for his existence. Young Pinneberg's efforts to establish himself in society end in miserable failure. The „little man" proves to be inadequately equipped to meet the exacting and vicious struggle for a spot in the sun in a capitalistic society filled with „sanierten Wirtschaftsführern". And Hans Fallada points to some of the reasons behind his failure and to the shortcomings of the „little man's" social status.

Pinneberg is a bookkeeper, he is a member of the white-collar class of the *Angestellten* who constitute the very backbone of that section of the *Kleinbürgertum* which is sometimes referred to as the *neue Mittelstand*. When Pinneberg's employer, aided by the constant threat of unemployment and a general crisis psychology, continues his constant intimidations and threats against him, Lämmchen believes that the only effective counteraction would be a demonstration of solidarity amongst the employees. But, alas, the „Solidarität aller Arbeitenden" in which

Lämmchen, the true daughter of a proletarian, so firmly believes, turns out to be an illusion and nonexistent amongst the members of Pinneberg's social class. When the decisive moment for joint-action on the part of the employees arrives, personal interests prove stronger than any desire to further a common cause and Pinneberg loses his position as a result. It is this lack of a sense of solidarity amongst the members of the white-collar class which constitutes what Hans Fallada considers to be one of its main characteristics and shortcomings. And it is this also which accounts for the acute lack of a sense of belonging and social identity which is one of the distinctive marks of Fallada's „little man". Pinneberg expresses his sense of insecurity bluntly and pitifully when he says: „Wir haben ewig Schiß."

The confrontation which Pinneberg has with his future parents-in-law, the proletarian Mörschels, serves well to further illustrate our point. Upon learning of Pinneberg's intention to marry her daughter, Frau Mörschel says to him:

„Was sind Sie denn? Können Sie denn überhaupt heiraten?"
„Ich bin Buchhalter. In einem Getreidegeschäft."
„Also Angestellter?"
„Ja."
„Arbeiter wäre mir lieber. – ..."
„... Mein Mädchen soll einfach bleiben." ... „Denken Sie nicht, daß sie was mitbekommt. Wir sind Proletarier. Bei uns gibt es das nicht." [2]

And Herr Mörschel points out the deficiencies of the white-collar class quite clearly when, having learned that Pinneberg receives no pay for his overtime work, he declares:

„Sehen Sie, darum wär mir ein Arbeiter für meine Tochter lieber: wenn mein Karl Überstunden macht, kriegt er sie bezahlt"
. . . .
„Warum krieg ich 'nen Schwiegersohn, dem sie nicht bezahlt werden?"
Pinneberg zuckt die Achseln.
„Weil ihr nicht organisiert seid, ihr Angestellten," erklärt ihm den

[2]   *Kleiner Mann – was nun?* (Berlin, Rowohlt Verlag, 1935), p. 18.

Fall Herr Mörschel. „Weil kein Zusammenhang ist bei euch, keine
Solidarität. Darum machen sie mit euch, was sie wollen."

. . . .

„Angestellter, wenn ich so was schon höre," sagt Mörschel. „Ihr
denkt, ihr seid was Besseres als wir Arbeiter." [3]

The shortcomings of the white-collar class, to which Mörschel
points, are not merely to be sought in the absence of representative and unifying organisations such as Trade Unions, set up
primarily for the purpose of achieving material ends. The lack
of a *Zusammenhang* amongst the members of the *Kleinbürgertum*
is above all a lack of a common spiritual bond, of a union of
common purposes and aspirations and of that unity which obliges
to mutual assistance and sympathy. And all this makes for the
atmosphere of infinite loneliness which surrounds Fallada's *Kleinbürger* and makes his plight all the more acute. The „little man"
has nothing to fall back on in times of need except his own
unstable self. Pinneberg realises his dilemma all too clearly when
he says to his wife: „Wir sitzen allein. Und die andern, die genau
so sind wie wir, die sitzen auch allein. Jeder dünkt sich was. Wenn
wir wenigstens Arbeiter wären! Die sagen Genosse zueinander
und helfen einander . . .".[4] Here, then, the „little man's" yearning
for a sense of social belonging and identity is made painfully clear.

Another incident which again sheds considerable light on the
lack of unity and social coherence amongst Fallada's *Kleinbürger*
is that which describes how Pinneberg, while attempting to secure
hospitalization funds for his wife, confronts a member of his own
social class and is made painfully aware of the gulf separating
them. The mere physical barrier of a counter, with Pinneberg
standing on the one side while one of his „colleagues" is seated
on the other, suffices to turn them into arch-enemies:

Ein Trost für Pinneberg, daß hinter der Barre Angestellte wie er
sitzen, Kollegen gewissermassen. Sonst könnte er ja ganz verzagt
werden inmitten dieser edlen Hölzer und Steine . . . Ein junger Mann

---

[3] *Ibid.*, pp. 20–21.
[4] *Ibid.*, p. 293.

sitzt da, beruhigend offen, nicht abgesperrt, nur an der anderen Seite
der Barre.

. . . .

Der junge Mann sieht Pinneberg an, Pinneberg sieht den jungen
Mann an. Sie sind beide recht anständig gekleidet, Pinneberg muß
das ja schon von Berufs wegen, sie sind beide sauber gewaschen und
rasiert, beide haben saubere Nägel und beide sind sie Angestellte.
Aber beide sind Feinde, Todfeinde, denn einer sitzt hinter der
Barriere und der andere steht davor. Der eine will, was er für sein
Recht hält, aber der andere hält es für eine Belästigung. [5]

And so in the end Pinneberg has to realise that the „Solidarität
der Angestellten" amounts to nothing more than a „Solidarität
des Neides gegen den Tüchtigen". Characteristically, it is the
intrigues of one of his „colleagues" which finally succeed in
bringing about his downfall and sweeping him out into the
turbulent mass of the unemployed. And in this sea of human
despair the „little man" fights for survival as a lonely and isolated
swimmer, with no rafts to cling to and but one safe haven in
view, that of his marriage, upheld and maintained by the sustaining power of the woman. We shall deal with the function of
marriage and the significant role of the woman in Fallada's world
of „little men" in our next chapter. It is important to note, however, that it is characteristic of Fallada's „little men" that they lack
any forms of alignments outside the confines of their private
lives. They are absolutely uncommitted politically, as indeed
Fallada himself always was. True enough, in *Kleiner Mann — was
nun?* communism is on various occassions hinted at as the only
feasible solution to the problems confronting the „little man".
Lämmchen displays open „Sympathien für die Kommunisten"
and Pinneberg, too, threatens to vote for the Communists in the
next election. But this is nothing more than the helpless and
indeed completely aimless gropings of someone who has never
really possessed the anchorage of a social and political identity
of any kind. The Pinnebergs never do join a political party. The
truth of the matter is that there is in fact no party in existence
for them to join; no party, at any rate, that they could consider

[5] *Ibid.,* pp. 250–251.

as even remotely concerned with the matter of representing the interest of their class. Hans Fallada himself certainly never considered communism, or let alone Nazism, which is mentioned briefly in *Kleiner Mann — was nun?*, as the answers to the predicament of his „little man". Indeed our author never concerned himself seriously with ephemeral political issues. In introducing the nonpolitical figure of the „little man" as the central character of his works, Fallada always keeps his eyes firmly fixed on the plight of the individual soul as such, asserting the humanity of his characters and thus introducing a truly universal and timeless element into his works.

Pinneberg's story in *Kleiner Mann — was nun?* ends with the social *Deklassierung* of the „little man". He becomes acutely aware of the degree of his degradation when, while wandering aimlessly through the city and dreading to return home, he is humiliated in public by a policeman, who chases him off the sidewalk and down the streets. Now the „little man" realises: „daß er draußen ist, daß er hier nicht mehr hergehört, daß man ihn zu Recht wegjagt: ausgerutscht, versunken, erledigt. Ordnung und Sauberkeit: es war einmal. Arbeit und sicheres Brot: es war einmal. Vorwärtskommen und Hoffen: es war einmal."[6] The note of defeatism and self-pity sounded here is a measure of the sense of fultility with which the „little man" views his lot in society.

We shall see that Pinneberg's fate is characteristic of the fates of many of Fallada's *Kleinbürger*. We shall also see that Hans Fallada recruited most of the more prominent members of his army of „little men" from the social class of which Pinneberg is the representative *par excellence,* indeed its very personification. The state of this class is one of flux and fragmentation in which it is difficult to determine whether the process is one of the formation of a distinctive social identity or of mere total dissolution. Fallada's „little man" is socially displaced, he is at home neither in the environment of the middle class bourgeoisie nor, as we have seen, in that of the proletariat. He appears, rather, to be the product of a process of amalgamation of certain ele-

---

[6] *Ibid.,* p. 343.

ments from both of these social classes. As a member of the *Kleinbürgertum* he is often, as a consequence of social and economic upheavals, brougt down to proletarian level and is, perhaps, best described as a middle class *déclassé*. Old Mörschel at one point quite correctly refers to Pinneberg's position as that of a person sitting „zwischen zwei Stühlen“. The „little man's“ social status is most aptly characterised by the term „Stehkragen-prolet“, which Pinneberg knows the proletarians apply to him.

Hans Fallada had himself been close to the real problems of the „Stehkragenprolet“, having held such positions as bookkeeper, newspaper propagandist, reporter, accountant and real estate agent. Consequently it was again with an insight of the first-hand order that he investigated the plight of the „Stehkragenprolet“. Jürgen Manthey has pointed out that Fallada also read with great interest a sociological study by Siegfried Kracauer entitled *Die Angestellten*, which may well have helped him to clarify and deepen his own ideas on and analysis of the social class of his „little man“.[7]

The first act of what one might, with some justification, call the tragedy of Fallada's „little man“ had in fact already been enacted in *Bauern, Bonzen und Bomben*, a book which attained a brilliance in its narrative vigour that Hans Fallada perhaps never quite equalled in his later works. It was with this novel that Fallada, after having kept silent for almost a decade following the publication of his first juvenile and expressionistic novels *Der junge Goedeschal (1920)* and *Anton und Gerda* (1923), re-entered the arena of German literature, this time to stay. In the midst of this gripping account of peasant disturbances and the dissent of political factions in a small town at the time of the Weimar Republic, Fallada unfolds the fateful story of the „little man“, Max Tredup. And it is the plight of this weak *Kleinbürger* to a much greater degree than the politics of the day, on which actually only passing and insignificant comments are made, that really concerns the author. Max Tredup, the unfortunate little newspaper propagandist and reporter, again is a member of the

---

[7] Jürgen Manthey, *op. cit.*, p. 88.

white-collar class. Like so many of Fallada's „little men" he, too,
represents a partial self-portrait of the author, who collected the
material on which the novel is based as a reporter in a political
lawsuit held in Neumünster in 1929. Tredup's desperate attempt
to assert himself in society ends in failure and a tragic death.
Here, then, the „little man's" inability to acquit himself of the
task of standing his ground in the competitive struggle for existence in a highly impersonal society already becomes quite evident.
Max Tredup is the first of the many luckless *Kleinbürger* whose
pathetic fates Hans Fallada was again and again to interpret in
his work. His existence is of a kind that seems almost preordained
to end in failure and total social rejection. Struggle as he may,
Max Tredup finds the path leading to his rightful place in society
strewn with a variety of insurmountable obstacles. At one point in
the novel we are told: „Tredup gehört nun einmal zu den
Menschen, die kein Glück haben." [8] Because Tredup realises
that this is indeed so, he resorts to fraudulent practices as the
last means of wresting a living from a society which proves too
unsympathetic towards his most basic needs. Tredup admits
freely to Stuff, the editor of the newspaper, that he considers
himself no longer fit for anything but „dirty work". But he
inevitably falls victim to his own „Dreckarbeit", which proves
to be too petty and ineffective to be able to really tip the scales
in any decisive way. Again the members of the white-collar class,
in stark contrast to the peasants, are pictured as being engaged
in ruthless competition with each other. Stuff's disillusioned
comment that „Kollegen sind immer das Schlimmste" proves to
be only too true when he finds himself the victim of the intrigues
of his „colleague", Tredup. Stuff, who is yet another version of
the stock figure of the „good guy", who appears so frequently
in most of Fallada's novels, avoids further conflict by simply
stepping down from his position. But even though the slanderous
rumours which Tredup has been circulating about Stuff do
succeed in removing Stuff and installing Tredup as the editor
of the „Chronik", Tredup's „success" turns out to be short-lived

[8] *Bauern, Bonzen und Bomben* (Berlin, Rowohlt Verlag, 1931), p. 462.

indeed. He, too, becomes an inevitable victim of the „Kampf aller gegen alle" and soon loses his newly gained position. The murder of Tredup brings to an end what is perhaps the most tragic career of all of Fallada's „little men".

Tredup's fate as well as that of Pinneberg point clearly and directly to the sorry lot of Willi Kufalt in *Wer einmal aus dem Blechnapf frißt* (1934), where we meet the „little man" again, this time in a prison cell. Tredup, incidentally, had also spent a brief period in jail. The plunge into total social degradation, which death in *Bauern, Bonzen und Bomben* and a happy marriage in *Kleiner Mann — was nun?* had prevented the „little man" from taking, now occurs in this powerful novel which Manthey, with some justification, believes to be „der beste Gefängnisroman im deutschen Sprachbereich".[9] With Willi Kufalt, the „beschattete Bruder des kleinen Mannes Pinneberg", as the author calls him in the preface, Hans Fallada introduces yet another version of his *Pechvogel*. This time it is his „little man", who had begun as a respectable clerk in an office, turned a little criminal as the result of adverse social and economic conditions. Willi Kufalt, faced with the pressing question: „Was nun?", which is so symptomatic of the plight of Fallada's „little man", has found an answer to it by sliding into crime. „Ein Ding drehen" becomes the last means to which the „little man" resorts in order to extract a living from an uncomprehending society. *Wer einmal aus dem Blechnapf frißt* is Hans Fallada's harshest criticism of bourgeois society and of its penal system which, by its very routine destroys all personal initiative and self-respect of the prisoner, thus contributing but very little to the betterment of the criminal and failing, above all, to equip the convict adequately for the difficult task of rehabilitation in society. The result of such punishment is not the prevention of further crimes but, rather, a fostering of an inevitable relapse into crime as the only means of wresting a living from a society whose stigma of social *Deklassierung* one bears. It is this which constitutes the basic theme of his realistic novel and which is, of course, already clearly indicated in the wording

9 Jürgen Manthey, *op. cit.*, p. 106.

of its title. Kufalt is, like Tredup and Pinneberg, a member of
the white-collar class. After his release from prison and upon
stepping out into a world he has not seen for many years, Kufalt
soon makes the painful experience that the little word *vorbestraft*
proves to be an indelible mark of social disgrace. And so we
accompany this „little man" on his distressing and disillusioning
journey which in the end turns out to have been nothing but a
vicious circle. Fallada again points to the acute lack of a sense
of solidarity and social identity amongst the members of the
white-collar class. The statement that „Kollegen sind immer das
Schlimmste", which Stuff makes in *Bauern, Bonzen und Bomben*
and which stands as the very formulation of this sorry lack of
social coherence amongst Fallada's „little men", is repeated by
the habitual criminal, Batzke, in *Wer einmal aus dem Blechnapf
frißt*. Batzke, who, similar to Stuff in *Bauern, Bonzen und Bomben*
or Heilbutt in *Kleiner Man – was nun?*, plays the familiar role
of the superior companion who occasionally and unexpectedly
is even capable of rising to an awareness of some sort of sense
of responsibility and who is, at any rate, the much-needed object
of the „little man's" tendency towards hero worship, warns Kufalt
in the following manner:

„Du hälst es ja doch nicht durch. Da strampelst du dich zwei Monate
ab oder drei oder fünf, und schiebst Kohldampf und rennst dich um
nach Arbeit. Und vielleicht kriegst du wirklich Arbeit und schuftest
dich tot, daß sie dich nur behalten. Aber dann kommt's doch
irgendwie raus, daß du gesessen hast, und der Chef befördert dich
an die Luft oder die Kollegen – die sind immer die schlimmsten –
wollen mit so'nem Verbrecher nicht arbeiten." [10]

The bitter truth of this warning soon becomes evident. No helping
hand from any quarter, and least of all from members of his
own social class, stretches out to aid the ex-convict in his painful
task of attempting to restore himself to good repute in society.
On various occasions Kufalt does seem to be on the way to
achieving his ambition to be in a position to live a free and
respectable life and even to marry and settle down. But all his at-

[10] *Wer einmal aus dem Blechnapf frißt* (Berlin, Rowohlt Verlag, 1934),
p. 46.

tempts to re-enter into a normal and ordered existence end in failure. Harsh social conventions, society's stigma of shame and his own lack of a strong will power turn the „little man's" problems into a vicious circle, making his recovery impossible. Driven about aimlessly, like a leaf in the autumn wind, and with nothing but his own handicapped self to fall back on, Willi Kufalt finally has to give up all hopes for help from his fellow beings: „Auf diesem schmerzvollen Weg, mit dem immer wieder versagenden Kopf hatte er zuerst den Gedanken aufgeben müssen an die Hilfe der Menschen: er war allein." [11] And so for Wilhelm Kufalt, whose fate is reminiscent of that of Zuckmayer's Wilhelm Voigt in more ways than one, there remains but one way out, namely a relapse into crime and the final humiliating but comforting acceptance of the prison as a safe haven which, once again, permits a life devoid of all responsibilities. Like so many of his pathetic brothers, Kufalt in the end displays an attitude of complete defeatism. Realizing that he lacks the self-reliance and confidence required to assert himself in society, he exclaims: „Was hatte Arbeiten, Demütigsein, Entbehren für einen Sinn, wenn man doch scheiterte?", thus echoing almost literally the outcry of his spiritual brother, Tredup: „Was spielen die mit ihm? Soll er nie Ruhe haben? Sich nie freuen dürfen? . . . Wozu sich Mühe geben? Es wird ja doch nichts mit ihm." [12] Time and again Fallada's „little men" are victims of social forces they do not fully comprehend. They become the mere dice in the hands of the more aggressive and ruthless members of a highly competitive society and are finally tossed away and left to decay „am Rande des Daseins". The majority of Hans Fallada's *Kleinbürger* become such pitiful social failures. They are declassed citizens or in the process of being declassed. Quite aptly Ruth Römer has referred to Fallada as to the „Dichter des kleinbürgerlichen Verfalls".[13] Our author was not only *the* poet of the *Kleinbürgertum* but also, and per-

---

[11] *Ibid.*, pp. 483–484.
[12] *Bauern, Bonzen und Bomben*, p. 435; *Wer einmal aus dem Blechnapf frißt*, p. 424.
[13] Ruth Römer, „Dichter des Kleinbürgerlichen Verfalls. Vor zehn Jahren starb Hans Fallada" *Neue Deutsche Literatur*, V (1957), Heft 2, 120.

haps first and foremost, the author of the decline and fall of the German *Kleinbürgertum* in the period between the two World Wars. No doubt Heinrich Spiero, in his all too brief comments on Hans Fallada in his *Geschichte des deutschen Romans* (1950), also has this fact in mind when he speaks of Fallada's work depicting „eine sinkende Schicht".[14]

In his starkly convincing and objective style and with a technique that has achieved his ideal of a *Dialogform* of which he speaks in *Heute bei uns zu Haus* and which, indeed, establishes him as a worthy successor to Fontane, Hans Fallada in *Wer einmal aus dem Blechnapf frißt* brings a world to view which we may aptly call the underworld of the *Kleinbürger*. Having demonstrated his inadequacy to assert himself in society, the „little man" is now relegated to the *Schattenseite* of humanity. But here, too, he remains the underdog he had been in society and never soars to any great heights of achievement. His crimes are petty and, just as he had in society, so here, too, he fails to achieve any degree of success. Willi Kufalt never develops the qualities that would make him a „successful" criminal; he remains lonely and insecure: „So geht's ihm immer. Wenn er mit anderen zusammen ist, redet er, erzählt er, gibt an, ist der große Ganove und allbefahrene Knastschieber, aber allein mit sich ist er sehr allein, wird klein und verzagt." [15] And so it is not the despondent „little man", Kufalt, but his self-confident and often ruthless „friend", Batzke, the „große Ganove", who undertakes the really „worthwhile" projects. Kufalt never gets around to „ein großes Ding zu drehen", and Batzke flatly declares him unreliable and unsuitable as a partner in the proposed jewelry robbery: „Höre einmal zu", sagte Batzke. „Ich habe mir die Sache überlegt. Das läßt sich machen. Aber ich möchte es ohne dich machen. Du taugst nicht zu so was." [16]

The shocking sequel to the tragic story of the „little man", Kufalt, was to be presented in one of Hans Fallada's most spiritless

---

[14] Heinrich Spiero, *Geschichte des deutschen Romans* (Berlin, Walter De Gruyter & Co., 1950), p. 563.
[15] *Wer einmal aus dem Blechnapf frißt*, p. 18.
[16] *Ibid.*, p. 434.

and morbid stories: *Der Trinker* (1950). It is here that the curtain finally falls on the tragedy of the decline and fall of the „little man“, which had begun with *Bauern, Bonzen und Bomben*. *Der Trinker*, written in the short period of just two weeks while the author was imprisoned, in 1944, on a charge of attempting to murder his first wife shortly after he had been divorced from her, is the story of a small businessman's gradual moral and physical decay. Characteristically, the experiences of Erwin Sommer, the drinker, are related in the first person and in diary form. Hans Fallada sketches every phase of a process of gradual degradation which begins with a first nip from a glass of wine and ends in dipsomania, crime, the disruption of a marriage and the eventual permanent confinement in a mental institution. Again it is the *Kleinbürger* who is the central figure in this terribly depressing tale. It is the story of the „*little man*“ who, like his brothers, Tredup, Pinneberg and Kufalt, had started his career as a little white-collar employee. But, unlike his unfortunate counterparts, Erwin Sommer had experienced a period of real success. He had seen the establishment of his own independent, small business and had even enjoyed the possession of his own home:

> Wir hatten uns aus Liebe geheiratet, damals waren wir alle beide sehr kleine Angestellte gewesen, jeder mit einem Handköfferchen, so waren wir zusammengelaufen. Ach, die herrliche entbehrungsreiche Zeit unserer ersten Ehejahre – wenn ich heute daran zurückdenke! ... Dann kam die wagemutige, von immerwährender Anspannung erfüllte Zeit, da ich mich selbständig machte, da ich mit Magdas Hilfe mein eigenes Geschäft aufbaute. Es glückte – o du lieber Himmel, wie uns damals alles glückte! [17]

For Hans Fallada *Glück* was always something to be regarded with a gread deal of suspicion. And in *Der Trinker*, as was to be expected, Erwin Sommer ultimately proves incapable of preserving his good fortune. When adverse conditions set in and threaten to jeopardise his position, the „little man“ simply cannot cope adequately with the ensuing pressures. And so he falls victim to

---

[17] *Der Trinker* (Hamburg, Rowohlt Verlag, 1959), p. 9.

the habit of drinking primarily because it provides him with the means to dull the perception of the actualities of everyday life and to elude the responsibilities and problems of his small business and, above all, those of his deteriorating marriage:

> Ich habe natürlich nicht immer getrunken, es ist sogar nicht sehr lange her, daß ich mit Trinken angefangen habe. Früher ekelte ich mich vor Alkohol; ... Aber dann kam eine Zeit, da es mir schlecht zu gehen anfing. Meine Geschäfte liefen nicht so, wie sie sollten, und mit den Menschen hatte ich auch mancherlei Mißgeschick. Ich bin immer ein weicher Mensch gewesen, ich brauchte die Sympathie und Anerkennung meiner Umwelt, wenn ich mir das auch nicht merken ließ und stets sehr selbstbewußt und sicher auftrat. Das Schlimmere war, daß ich das Gefühl bekam, auch meine Frau wende sich von mir ab. [18]

Erwin Sommer's characterisation of himself as a „weicher Mensch" is typical of all of Fallada's „little men". It is indicative of the fact that many of their problems have their roots equally as much in inner conflicts as in any adverse outer conditions. And for many of these *Pechvögel* alcohol becomes the last refuge.

In the end Erwin Sommer, the „kleiner, mittelmäßiger, entgleister Kaufmann", is discarded as „gemeingefährlich" and left to conclude his life as a brushmaker amongst the „letzte Ausschuß der Menschheit". Deprived of that little mark of social respectability, the *Herr* in front of his name, this most pathetic member of Falada's army of „little men" becomes a menace to society and joins the other social outcasts whose terrible lot it is to lead a life of permanent incarceration in some institution, cut adrift from the rest of „healthy" society. Sommer, too, like so many of his unfortunate brothers, is the victim of forces he does not fully understand:

> Es fängt immer mit etwas Kleinem an, und dann verstrickt es uns, es wächst riesengroß auf über uns – und durch Gitter sehen wir nur noch die Freiheit. Die Turmuhr schlägt die Stunden, Hunderte, Tausende, Zehntausende – umsonst! Der Wind weht aus Nord, aus Ost, aus Süd und West, er weht weich und bitterkalt – nicht für uns mehr – nie für uns! Ach, daß wir wissend gewesen wären! [19]

[18] *Ibid.*, p. 5.
[19] *Ibid.*, p. 164.

Ultimately for Erwin Sommer there remains but the intense wish and hope that death will soon release him of an existence that has become utterly meaningless and intolerable. An oppressive atmosphere of terrible pessimism and defeatism is all that remains at the end of this somber record of a downtrodden soul.

We may ask why Hans Fallada chose to portray so many of his „little men" as social failures and declassed citizens. There can be no doubt, that the experience of his own expulsion, at an early age, from the security of a well-to-do upper-middle class family and many of his subsequent harsh experiences, including periods of imprisonment, lie at the root of most of our author's writings. Seldom has an author revealed so much of his own inner self as did Hans Fallada in his literature of the plight of the „little man". Seldom, indeed, does D. H. Lawrence's famous remark that „one sheds one's sicknesses in books" find a more appropriate and revealing illustration. Anyone who has perused Fallada's autobiographical accounts related in *Heute bei uns zu Haus*, will realise immediately that the tragic story of his „little man", whether his name is Tredup, Pinneberg, Kufalt or Sommer, is at the same time and to a great degree the author's own life-story. In *Heute bei uns zu Haus* Fallada recalls the frustrating early years of his career with words that strike up an all too familiar note: „Ich war mittlerweile fünfunddreißig Jahre alt geworden und hatte eingesehen, daß sich alles Abstrampeln nicht lohnte. Ich hatte eben kein Glück. Wozu sich anstrengen? In meinen Papieren stand von Geburt an: Pechvogel."[20] It was, no doubt, the painful realization that he was such a *Pechvogel* which prompted Rudolf Ditzen to discard his respectable name and to write his books under the rather ominous name of the unfortunate oracular horse in one of Grimm's fairy tales.

In *Der eiserne Gustav* (1938) Fallada once again depicted his „little man", not so much in the figure of Iron Gustav himself but rather in that of his youngest son, Heinz Hackendahl. After the Second World War Hans Fallada, incidentally, disavowed *Der eiserne Gustav*, which is the only work wherein the author

---

[20] *Heute bei uns zu Haus*, p. 8.

finally succumbed to the demands of the Hitler regime to work into his fiction the Nazi interpretation of post-World War I German history. How unsuccessful his endeavours to please the National Socialists were, may be illustrated by the fact that, in 1943, his books, including *Der eiserne Gustav*, were pronounced „undesirable". Peter W. Tügel undertook to free the novel „von den Schlacken der dreißiger Jahre", as we are told in the epilogue to the edition of the book which appeared in 1958. It is in the form of this „cleansed" version that the novel has once again become available to the reading public. The Blüchert publishing company in Hamburg, which published the novel, has also now acquired the publication rights for all of Fallada's works.

Der eiserne Gustav is in a very real sense the *Buddenbrooks* o fthe *Kleinbürgertum*. Here the process of disintegration of the *Kleinbürgertum* is recorded through the history of a family. The book, which covers the years from 1914 to about 1930 and gives a very vivid portrayal of all the important historical events of that period, is an account of the decay of a lower-middle class family, dominated by the paralysing influence of a die-hard Prussian, the cab-owner, „Iron Gustav". There can be no doubt that Fallada's own extremely strained and disturbed relation to his father lies at the root of the portrayal of this tyrant's oppressive sway over his children. In the figure of Heinz Hackendahl, the youngest member of this unfortunate family, which Heinz at one point calls a „dekadente Familie" and which ends up in total fragmentation, with a sister sliding into prostitution, a brother into speculation in the inflation and old Hackendahl himself into utter poverty, Fallada once again returns to his „little man". Heinz Hackendahl is in many ways the re-embodiment of Johannes Pinneberg. Like Pinneberg he, too, is a member of the *Kleinbürgertum*. He, too, loses his position as a bank clerk at the peak of unemployment and passes through the same demoralising experiences which Pinneberg had to endure. He, too, joins the army of the destitute, who tread the streets for countless miles in an aimless search for employment. In *Der eiserne Gustav* the tone is heightened to one of bitter hatred and hopeless despair. Intense antagonisms develop between the unemployed and the

employed, who are merely employed because others are unemployed. The *Stempelstelle* is the focal point of this bitter enmity.
Here again members of the white-collar class confront each other
as irreconcilable foes, with one party standing on the receiving
side of the counter, while the other is seated on the donating side:
„Ja, du Glotzauge hinter dem Schalter, dich meine ich! Hast
du schon deine Kinder abends vor Hunger blarren hören, du
Speckjäger, und hast keine Krume Brot mehr und keinen Pfennig,
was zu kaufen!" [21] And so in the end the „little man", Heinz
Hackendahl, realises that he has become a „paria", forced to
live amongst „den Grauen, den Elendsgestalten" and banished
to the „Nachtseite" of life with his only function being reduced
to that of „stempeln gehen". In the original version of the novel,
Hans Fallada permitted his nonpolitical figure of the „little man"
to seek a solution to his „was nun?" by joining the Nazi Party.
No one who is acquainted with Fallada's whole work could possibly
fail to notice and feel how badly out of tune such a „solution"
is with the author's general outlook and true intentions. Moreover,
if Harry Slochower's excellent interpretation of the fairy tale
Märchen vom Stadtschreiber, der aufs Land flog (1935) is correct
– as we believe it to be – then Hans Fallada had already, for those
who could see through the camouflage, presented his views on
Nazidom and its disastrous effects on his „little man" three years
before the publication of *Der eiserne Gustav*. Harry Slochower
believes this complicated story to be in fact a brilliant satire on
the „brown magic" and „double bookkeeping" of Nazidom. He
interprets the tale of the transformation, by means of a brown
hair, of the little bank clerk, Guntram Spatt, into a „free" sparrow
and his subsequent perplexing experiences, most disturbing of which
is that every person he meets seems to have two faces, as „depicting the split character and ambiguity of the forces around the
little man, producing an inner war within him". And he continues:
„It is the story of the „brown" magic used to give him the illusion
of liberty, while actually keeping him bound. [22] It is quite certain

[21] *Der eiserne Gustav* (Hamburg, Blüchert Verlag, 1958), p. 649.
[22] Harry Slochower, „Hauptmann and Fallada: Uncoordinated Writers
of Nazi Germany", *Accent*, III (1942), 23.

that Fallada's *Kleinbürger* felt more perplexed and more acutely at a loss when faced with the forces of National Socialism than he had ever been during the upheavals of the Weimar Republic. In *Kleiner Mann – großer Mann, alles vertauscht* (1939) Hans Fallada again depicts his „little man". In this novel, which bears the subtitle „Max Schreyvogels Last und Lust des Geldes", the author shows the „little man" fully exposed to the destructive forces of capitalism and deals with a problem that concerned him again and again. It is the question of the important role which money plays as a lever of social prestige and power, and its special significance in the lives of the „little men". This is a recurrent theme in Fallada's work and we might do well to discuss it briefly at this juncture.

Money almost casts a magic spell on Fallada's characters, and he has portrayed men under this spell on numerous occassions: Wolfgang Pagel, the passionate gambler in *Wolf unter Wölfen* (1937); Erich Hackendahl, the ruthless speculator and profiteer in *Der eiserne Gustav*, and many more like them. Both of these men are shown in that bewildering period of the great German Inflation, when money as a common measure of value crumbled. For Fallada's „little men" money is first and foremost the absolutely indispensable and much-needed instrument required to fulfil their most basic daily needs, and as such an essential means of survival it is a factor that remains ever present in their minds and haunts their very dreams. Max Tredup in *Bauern, Bonzen und Bomben* falls victim to his desperate attempt to secure a little extra cash and so, indeed, does his brother, Willi Kufalt. In *Kleiner Mann – was nun?* Fallada covers one whole page with figures representing Lämmchen's tight monthly budget. He does the same thing in „100 Mark und ein fröhliches Weihnachtsfest", a short story contained in *Gesammelte Erzählungen*. Here a whole page is covered with the figures that make up the Christmas shopping list of a young *kleinbürgerliche* couple. In *Wolf unter Wölfen* Studmann speaks for all „little men" when he says:

Geld, das ist einfach das, was man zum Leben braucht, die Basis des Da-Seins, das Brot, das wir jeden Tag essen müssen, um da zu sein, der Anzug, den wir tragen müssen, um nicht zu erfrieren ...

. . . .

Ich habe entdeckt, daß neunundneunzig Prozent der Menschen sich
sehr um das Geld quälen müssen, daß sie Tag und Nacht daran
denken, davon reden, es einteilen, sparen, wieder anfangen – kurz,
daß Geld das ist worum sich die Welt dreht. Daß es einfach lächer-
lich lebensfremd ist, nicht an das Geld zu denken, nicht davon reden
zu wollen – das wichtigste, was es gibt! [23]

One might be tempted to interpret statements such as this one
as an avowal of an unconditional materialism. But evidence from
many of Fallada's works and particularly from one of his autobiographical novels and from the essay „Wie ich Schriftsteller
wurde", shows that he considered money to be one of the great
menaces to human happiness and inner peace. Money is seen as
the great tempter and its possession becomes a predominantly
moral concern to the individual. On the occasion of the overwhel-
ming success of *Kleiner Mann – was nun?*, which turned him
into a wealthy man overnight, Hans Fallada writes:

Die Gefahren, die uns von außen drohen, sind gering gegen die aus
unserm Innern. Wir selbst bereiten uns immer wieder die größten
Überraschungen. Der Kleine Mann wurde ein Welterfolg – ich muß
leider sagen: leider. Das Geld strömte nur so herbei. Wir hatten
von zweihundertzwanzig Mark glücklich gelebt, unsere Sorgen fingen
an, als wir plötzlich über große Summen zu verfügen hatten. Suses
Sorgen fingen da an, ich selbst verlor völlig den Kopf ... Ich gab das
Geld auf die sinnloseste Weise aus, es konnte ja nicht alle werden ...
Ich bekam für mein Geld nichts anderes als Kopfschmerzen, Arbeits-
unlust, Reue, Gewissensbisse. [24]

It was, no doubt, this experience which was later to provide the
central theme of *Kleiner Mann – großer Mann, alles vertauscht.*
The belief that the mere possession of sufficient money is not
the panacea for the problems facing the „little man" had already
been hinted at in *Kleiner Mann – was nun?* when Lämmchen
declares: „Geld hilft zu gar nichts. Arbeit würde helfen, ein
bißchen Hoffnung würde dem Jungen helfen. Geld Nein." [25] Then

---

[23] *Wolf unter Wölfen* (Berlin, Rowohlt Verlag, 1937), I. 86.
[24] *Heute bei uns zu Haus*, pp. 34–35.
[25] *Kleiner Mann – was nun?*, pp. 347–348.

in *Kleiner Mann –großer Mann, alles vertauscht,* the counterpart to *Kleiner Mann –was nun?,* Fallada confirmed this conviction by introducing the great servitude of money as the central theme and at the same time illustrating his somewhat muddled and contradictory views on capitalism. In this novel we find the „little man" miraculously transfored into a capitalist, who finds himself in the possession of millions bequeathed to him by an obscure uncle. We see how Max Schreyvogel, the somewhat naive little insurance clerk, proves himself unable to cope sensibly with his wealth. He simply takes it as the signal for an uninhibited and disastrous slide down the path of depravity. Schreyvogel's experiences are, again characteristically, narrated in the first person. Hans Fallada shows how money becomes a destructive and alienating force, capable of disrupting all human bonds and contributing to the fragmentation of society and the dismal isolation of the individual. Already in *Bauern, Bonzen und Bomben* Fallada had demonstrated how money constitutes a grave threat to the private life of the „little man". Money alienates Max Tredup from his wife and threatens to disrupt the last refuge of the „little man" in a ruthlessly competitive society: his marriage. In *Kleiner Mann – großer Mann, alles vertauscht* the same conclusion is reached:

Wenn bisher von den Verwirrungen erzählt wurde, die von außen auf uns eindrangen, muß ich jetzt von den Zerstörungen berichten, die das Geld in mir anrichtete. Sie waren so schlimm, daß sie sehr bald mein ganzes Verhältnis zu Karla veränderten, ja schließlich den Bestand unserer Ehe bedrohten. Bisher haben wir alles so ziemlich gemeinsam ertragen, jetzt trennen sich unsere Wege, und ich darf nur noch von mir erzählen. Denn auch dies ist ein Fluch des Geldes: daß es seinen Besitzer einsam macht und alle menschlichen Bande gefährdet. [26]

Money, then, may become the cause of the ruin of human relationships which are the very cornerstones of society. If, as we have seen, the „little man", as a member of the white-collar class, lacks any sense of social communion with the other members of

[26] *Kleiner Mann – großer Mann, alles vertauscht* (Hamburg, Blüchert Verlag, 1959), p. 181.

his class, the possession of money brings about an even more critical isolation. The conclusion that is finally reached is simply that „nichts macht so schnell satt – und satt heißt alt – wie das Geld"; and once again it is the „little man's" wife who saves him from complete disintegration and who insists: „daß Geld überhaupt nichts mit Glück zu tun hat – wenigstens solche Menchen wie wir können sich mit Geld überhaupt kein Glück kaufen!" [27]

One can hardly quarrel with the author over the relevance of his critique of the dangers to the moral integrity of the individual inherent in capitalism. It is, however, less fortunate to see Fallada's criticism linked with views which are so obviously untenable. For he can no longer claim to be coping plausibly with the problems confronting his „little man" when he sidesteps any further searching analysis by simply handing him a tranquilizing pill in the form of such unrealistic statements as: „daß Geld überhaupt nichts mit Glück zu tun hat", and offering him solace in the rather naive assurance that „wenigstens solche Menschen wie wir können sich mit Geld überhaupt kein Glück kaufen!" How contradictory these views are to those we heard expressed in *Wolf unter Wölfen*, where money is described as a necessary means of survival for the „little man", is only too clear. Surely in *Kleiner Mann – großer Mann, alles vertauscht*, in working out his main hypothesis: „Wie ein armer Mensch, ein kleiner Mann, versuchte Millionär zu sein, und es gelang ihm nicht",[28] Hans Fallada overshoots his mark considerably and lets a romantic vision of uncomplicated self-fulfilment and protected simplicity get the better of him. But perhaps we should not forget that the book was written and published in Hitler's Germany. The pressures of the totalitarian regime weighed heavily on Hans Fallada's mind, muffling his true self and causing him to shy away from the interpretation of problematic situations and the presentation of objective reality. It was only too often that he felt compelled to escape into a romantic area of naive and, indeed, rather irresponsible specula-

[27] *Ibid.*, p. 211.
[28] *Ibid.*, p. 228.

tion. Many of Fallada's novels which appeared during the Third Reich bear the mark of the almost unbearable strain under which they were written. Harry Slochower, in the aforementioned article, points to the „tortured" and „masochistic" symbolism occurring in such works as *Wir hatten mal ein Kind* (1934), *Wolf unter Wölfen* and *Märchen vom Stadtschreiber, der aufs Land flog*. Quite often the fairy tale remained Fallada's last refuge in a time too ruthlessly intolerant to permit the writing of works that have the force of documentaries.

After the collapse of the Nazi dictatorship, Hans Fallada began to breathe freely again. Once again he shed all his sicknesses in a frank self-analysis, which he called „eine Krankheitsgeschichte": *Der Alpdruck* (1947). Then, freed of the dross, he mustered his creative powers for the production of his last, great novel: *Jeder stirbt für sich allein* (1947). In this novel Fallada once again returns to his „little man". But in the figure of Otto Quangel the author presents us with a radically changed „little man". No longer is it the timid, weak and defeatist *Kleinbürger* of Fallada's earlier novels. Here for the first, last and only time, the „little man" is able to maintain his human dignity in the face of cruel adverse conditions. For once the „little man" appears in truly glorious splendour, the torchbearer of human integrity. Otto Quangel's decision to resist the rule of terror of the *Führerstaat* in his own small but determined way by depositing cards with anti-government slogans on them in frequently used places in public buildings, and his and his wife's subsequent refusal to bow their minds and bodies to the regime in order to escape certain death, represents a bold and heroic answer to the question: „Was nun?". No longer does the „little man" resign himself to his fate with the conviction that he is doomed to failure from the very outset. It is with the firm belief that: „Umsonst geschieht nichts in dieser Welt, und da wir gegen die rohe Gewalt für das Recht kämpfen, werden wir am Schluß doch die Sieger sein",[29] as the conductor, Dr. Reichhardt, puts it in prison, that Otto Quangel, unbroken in spirit to the very bitter end, walks to the machine

[29] *Jeder stirbt für sich allein* (Berlin, Aufbau Verlag, 1949), p. 458.

that will end his life. Hans Fallada's last interpretation of his „little man" presents him, not as the disintegrating, anti-heroic *Kleinbürger*, but as a true hero. This book gives convincing evidence that Fallada was in the process of regaining his old stature and attaining an even more positive clarity of vision. Fallada himself states in „Wie ich Schriftsteller wurde", in which he gives a detailed account of the genesis of this novel that took him just 24 days to write, that he felt convinced that he had once again succeeded in writing a book which could be regarded as being fully „gelungen". Then an early tragic death silenced our author forever.

Johannes R. Becher, in a tribute to Hans Fallada, makes the following comments:

Er war, was den Reichtum und die Vielartigkeit seiner Figuren anbelangt, wohl der bedeutendste der lebenden deutschen Erzähler ... Er verfügte über die breiteste Skala menschlicher Empfindung ... Die verborgensten Gefühle schlug er an, und nichts Unbewußte fehlte auf seiner Tastatur, und das Außergewöhnliche und Problematische wußte er verständlich und zugänglich zu machen in einer schlichten, volkstümlichen Sprache. Seine Liebe aber galt dem einfachen Leben und den kleinen Leuten. Daß das einfache Leben oft höchst kompliziert war und was an Großem in diesen kleinen Leuten träumte, das schilderte er uns meisterhaft. Er kannte sich in dem Leben dieser kleinen Leute aus wie kaum einer ... Von Fallada war immer, insofern er geneigt war, sich offen zu äußern, zuverlässig zu erfahren, wie der kleine Mann denkt .... Wenn wir von Fallada sprechen als von einem „Stück Deutschland", so ist dieses Stück nicht das beste und nicht das schlechteste. Es ist jene Menschenart, die heute, bei gewissen politischen Übertriebenheiten, wieder unberücksichtigt bleibt. [30]

The „Stück Deutschland" of which Becher speaks and which he correctly characterises as a segment of German society once again being grossly neglected, is what Hans Fallada would have called the *Stehkragenproletariat*. As we have seen, Fallada's *Kleinbürger* is a nonpolitical figure, who is indeed liable to be ignored „bei gewissen politischen Übertriebenheiten". The „little man" lacks

[30] Johannes R. Becher, „Was nun? Zu Hans Falladas Tod", *Aufbau*, (1947), Heft 2, 96—98.

a sense of class consciousness and has no political ideals to which he owes his allegiance. In choosing this figure as his central character, Hans Fallada, while analysing the peculiar problems confronting the „little man" and his social class, was able at the same time to concentrate his attention on what was always his main concern: the plight of the individual human being as such. This is what really matters for Fallada every time. It is clear that his writings of social criticism are, consequently, never merely social. As a critic of contemporary society, Hans Fallada always demonstrates his deeply involved and unbiased humanity, concerning himself with certain individual human problems which transcend all times and make for that truly universal element in his works of which we spoke earlier.

In *Wolf unter Wölfen* we read the following revealing conversation between the ex-officer, von Prackwitz, and his old friend, Studmann:

Aber was bist du denn? fragte von Prackwitz. Zu irgendeiner Gruppe oder Partei mußt du doch schließlich gehören.
Wieso? fragte von Studmann. Warum muß ich das eigentlich? Ja, ich weiß nicht, sagte von Prackwitz, ein wenig verblüfft. Zu irgendwas gehört doch schließlich jeder von uns, das ist doch schon wegen der Wahlen. Irgendwie muß man sich doch einordnen, ins Glied treten. Es ist gewissermaßen – ordentlich!
Wenn es für mich aber noch keine Ordnung gibt? fragte von Studmann. [31]

For Hans Fallada, too, there was no clearly defined *Ordnung* to which he could have offered his service. The only party to which he owed his wholehearted and unreserved allegiance and for which he time and again demonstrated his willingness to fight, was the party of humanity. In his books there is always a nonpartisan objectivity; there is a realism of the kind that does not ignore the joys in even the most distressed existence, even at the risk of appearing to be „sentimental". There is also simplicity of expression and, above all, a warmhearted, genuine and deeprooted sympathy, devoid of all sensationalism. But there is never an explicit didactic message other than that which proclaims

[31] *Wolf unter Wölfen*, I, 87.

concern for humanity's well-being. And all of this is in perfect
accord with Hans Fallada's artistic convictions and intentions. In
Heute bei uns zu Haus the author states his position as that of
a „kühler Beobachter" quite explicitly: „Ich, der ich vor mir
immer die These verfochten habe, der Autor dürfe in seinen
Büchern nicht mit Lob, nicht mit Tadel, nicht mit Erklärungen zu
spüren sein, jeder Leser müsse sich selbst sein Urteil bilden . . ." [32]
In the same novel Fallada names the one element in his writings
that always mattered most to him:

Es ist – trotz allem, wegen allem – herrlich, über Papier gebeugt zu
sitzen und von dem größten aller Wunder, dem Menschen, zu schreiben, meinethalben auch einmal von sich.
. . . .
Und dann: ich bin fünfzig, und alles mildert sich.
. . . .
Ich habe all mein Lebtage Menschen gefressen, ich habe sie mit ihren
Bewegungen, Redensarten, Gefühlen in meinem Gehirn notiert, und
da habe ich sie nun jederzeit parat zu sofortigem Gebrauch! Nichts
hat mich so interessiert wie die Erkenntnis, warum Menschen so
handeln wie sie handeln . . . Dies hat die Natur in mich gelegt, und
mir dadurch die Grundlage, den Stoff für all meine Schreiberei
gegeben . . . [33]

It was characters, then, and not ideas that were always Hans
Fallada's prime concern. He sought to understand and interpret
man's limitations and all the complex reasons behind human
actions and he strove, above all, to approach all problems with
an adjusted and a truly objective attitude. It is in this manner
that Fallada succeeds in bringing the plight of his characters close
to our hearts and in portraying his „little man" as a human being
whose feelings and problems demand and, indeed, receive our
sympathy and understanding.

[32]   *Heute bei uns zu Haus,* p. 203.
[33]   *Ibid.,* p. 210 and p. 252.

II

MARRIAGE AND THE ROLE OF WOMAN

One of the issues of man's social life which repeatedly proved of paramount concern to Hans Fallada was the important function which the basic human bond and social institution of marriage performs in society and particularly in the world of his „little men". Even though on some occasions he does depict other family relationships, it is always primarily the marital relationship on which he attempts to shed light. The theme of marriage crops up in almost all of Fallada's major novels. Coupled with this theme is yet another, complementary and even more significant one for Hans Fallada, namely that of the role played by the woman in the marital relationship and in society at large. These are the kind of „social" problems to which our author devoted his main attention.

Our aim in this chapter, then, is to discuss Fallada's interpretation of the relations of husband and wife and to see what importance he attaches to the function of marriage in the social life of his „little man". At the same time we shall attempt to show how he time and again assigns significant roles to his female characters. We shall see that the image of the loving, strong-willed and characterful woman dominates almost every one of Fallada's novels, and particularly those that deal with happy marital relations. H. A. Wyk in his comments on the figure of Lämmchen in *Kleiner Mann –was nun?* quite aptly states that:

It is not yet a threadbare phrase to say that this character ... represents the return of the tender and all-bountiful love of woman; she is a marvelously simple, profoundly human Madonna conception, diffusing a clarity of heart through which men again perceive woman as the essence of the community and the guardian of its enduring values. [1]

Perusing Hans Fallada's autobiographical tale *Heute bei uns zu Haus*, the reader is constantly made aware of the fact that our author clearly considered his marriage – his first one, in this case – to have been the most decisive event of his life. He admits freely that it was his wife, and she alone, who was able to dispel the clouds of complete hopelessness and disillusionment which engulfed and threatened to smother him completely, and it was she who played the key role in his subsequent rise to success. The whole book is, in fact, dedicated to his wife, Suse, and its first chapter begins with a frank confession of gratitude to her, written in the following sincere words:

Am Anfang und am Ende dieses Buches und auf allen seinen übrigen Seiten ist von meiner Frau Suse die Rede – auch wo nicht von ihr gesprochen wird. Sie erst hat mich zu dem gemacht, was ich geworden bin, sie hat einen Verbummelten wieder das Arbeiten gelehrt, einen Hoffnungslosen die Hoffnung. Durch ihren Glauben, ihre Treue, ihre Geduld wurde aufgebaut, was wir heute besitzen, was uns alle Tage freut. Und das alles geschah ohne viele Worte, ohne Aufhebens, ohne Schulmeisterei, einfach dadurch, daß sie da war, daß sie in guten und schlimmen Stunden zu mir hielt. Daß sie an mich glaubte. Daß sie so war, wie sie war. Güte und Geduld und Verzeihenkönnen, auch wo sie nicht verstand. [2]

And later in the book Fallada admits that in all their mutual struggles through „dick und dünn", it was always his wife who bore the „Hauptlast" of the adversities.

Hans Fallada was married twice. The tragic breakup of his first, extremely happy marital union was caused by Fallada's involvement in the situation of the eternal triangle.[3] The portrait of his second wife in *Der Alpdruck* gives evidence of the fact that, despite its struggles and many trying times, his second marriage, too, nevertheless provided Fallada with the support and anchorage he always needed so sorely. It was, then, as a person

---

[1] H. A. Wyk, „Hans Fallada", *The Living Age*, CCCXLIV (1933), 329.
[2] *Heute bei uns zu Haus, p.* 7.
[3] For futher details see: Jürgen Manthey, *op. cit.*, pp. 142ff.

who had found marriage a great, though never easily won, blessing that Hans Fallada wrote about the relations of husband and wife. And it was also as a husband who had experienced the reassuring and steadying influence of the loving and courageous wife that Fallada depicted the role of the woman in matrimony. Consequently, it is primarily with happy marriages, with marital concord rather than with marital antagonisms, that our author chiefly deals in his works. In the end, love prevails in almost every one of his major novels. Hans Fallada did, however, write a few novels which depict the miseries of unhappy marriages. And these books serve to accentuate, by way of contrast, the necessity and value of harmonious marital relationships. We shall now first turn our attention to those of Hans Fallada's novels that depict marital discord.

In *Wir hatten mal ein Kind* Fallada for the first time dealt with marital misery and its disastrous consequences. The book is the story of a ruthless young farmer, Johannes Gäntschow, whose background is an island in the Baltic Sea. Young Gäntschow marries Elise Schmitt, a young teacher he had met while spending a few *Wanderjahre* in various cities and on manorial estates in the province. Upon their return to the island, the newly married couple soon runs into marital difficulties. Fallada develops his theme with the aid of the eternal triangle plot of husband, wife and a third person. The third in this case is Gäntschow's old *Jugendliebe,* Christiane Fidde. Both Chritiane and Elise are loving and characterful women, imbued with all the qualities of Fallada's most lovable female characters. But the ruthless egotist, Johannes Gäntschow, proves unworthy of the love of either of them. When he finally deserts his wife and elopes with Christiane, it is only to prove his inability to build a happy union even with the woman he had always believed himself to be deeply in love with. Gäntschow's union with Christiane, too, ends in tragedy, with the death of their child and the rueful return of Christiane to her alienated husband. Love no longer prevails and marital antagonisms lead to disaster for all parties concerned. Elise, a perfectly lovable character and one of those gentle beings who possess that unique gift of being able to conceal their strongest feelings, again and again attempts to win the love and confidence of her husband, believing that „einen Menschen muß auch er haben". But she fails, and when finally she has to realise her betrayal, her love turns to hatred and jealousy and she resolves upon revenge. In her husband's absence she lays waste to their farm. Then she leaves, never to be heard of again. And so at the end of this immensely long story, which Fallada with some justification believed to be one of his best books, Johannes Gäntschow, whose character has alienated him from everyone, even from the only two people who really loved him, stands in utter isolation realising that: „Er hatte sie nie geliebt. Er hatte nie einen Menschen auf der Erde geliebt, er hatte nur sich geliebt"[4]

At one point in the novel Hans Fallada declares: „Ehen sind die verletzlichsten Dinge von der Welt, wirkliche Ehen, heißt das." And in this case the author places the blame for the disruption of the fragile treasure of a marriage squarely on the shoulders of the man. Johannes Gäntschow resents the domination of the loving woman in marriage, which Hans Fallada always suggests is an absolutely essential element of a happy union. Gäntschow refuses stubbornly to be moulded by his wife's love and to sacrifice part of his individuality for the sake of a happy alliance. Even before his marriage to Elise, we are told that Gäntschow was bent on avoiding intrusions into his self-sufficiency: „Aber er wollte nicht. Er wollte sich behalten. Er wollte erst einmal er selbst werden, ehe er sich hingab, und vielleicht war es sogar möglich, so sehr er selbst zu werden, daß man bei aller späteren Hingabe sich nie aufgab, hingab, in andere Hände gab."[5] – „Sich hingeben – sich in andere Hände geben,, is precisely what Gäntschow refuses to do later in his marriage. And thus he fails to fulfil what Hans Fallada considered to be the barest essentials for a happy marital union. At the bottom of his heart Gäntschow, in fact, despises all women, considering them to be too emotional and without reason. In this respect he stands in complete contrast to such figures as Pinneberg Tredup or Kufalt. Gäntschow de-

---

[4] *Wir hatten mal ein Kind* (Berlin, Rowohlt Verlag, 1934), p. 538.
[5] *Ibid.,* p. 241.

spises the love of Elise from the very outset: „Ihre Liebe macht sie scharfsichtig, sie besitzt nicht Verstand – den besitzen Frauen nie, davon ist er fest überzeugt." [6] Unlike a figure like Pinneberg, Gäntschow will never admit that he needs the support and understanding of his wife. At one point, in a violent outburst, he tells Elise brutally: „Ich habe dir von eh und je gesagt, daß ich kein Ehemann bin, kein Ehemann werde. Ich tue, was ich will." [7] Here, indeed, man no longer perceives woman as the „essence of the community". And for Hans Fallada the disastrous consequences are only too apparent. No redeeming forces of any kind remain for Gäntschow and his decline becomes inevitable.

In *Ein Mann will hinauf* (first published in serial form in 1941; appeared in book form in 1953) Fallada again depicts marital antagonisms. This time he describes an ambitious and ruthless young parvenu, Karl Siebrecht, mismated with a simple yet characterful woman. Siebrecht fails in marriage basically for the same reasons that had led to Johannes Gäntschow's failure. He, too, is too coldhearted an egotist and individualist to make a good husband. Again Fallada introduces the triangular plot to develop his theme. When Karl meets Hertha Eich, a sophisticated and refined woman, the contrast between her and his plain wife, Rieke, makes him aware of how great, too, the disparity is between himself and his wife:

Karl Siebrecht aber schämte sich, er schämte sich seiner Frau. Plötzlich hörte sein Ohr wieder diese gemeine Sprache, und wer so gemein redete, der dachte auch gemein.
„Es ist Schluß, Rieke", sagte er. „Kommen Sie, Fräulein Eich, ich bringe Sie noch heraus." ...
„Es tut mir sehr leid ...", sagte das junge Mädchen.
„Ihnen muß nichts leid tun, Sie haben es gut gemeint", antwortete er.
„Es war schon vorher alles kaputt, dies gab nur den letzten Anstoß."
„Trotzdem!" beharrte Hertha sich. Sie betrachtete ihn nachdenklich.
„Es ist schade", meinte sie dann. „Ihre Frau liebt Sie."
„Was hilft mir das? Ich liebe sie nicht, und wir passen auch nicht zueinander. Ich habe es nie so gefühlt wie eben, als ich Sie beide nebeneinander sah." [8]

[6]   *Ibid.*, p. 288.
[7]   *Ibid.*, p. 390.
[8]   *Ein Mann will hinauf* (München, Südverlag, 1953), p. 401.

A divorce is finally secured and both partners seek solace in remarriage. But whereas Rieke's second marriage turns out to be a happy union, Karl's never develops beyond that degree of familiarity and mutual affection which permits his second wife, Hertha, to refer to him simply as to „mein Freund". It is interesting to note in this connection that, although a number of Fallada's characters do embark upon a second marriage, the whole problem of remarriage is never fully elaborated upon by the author.

Hans Fallada was always intent on revealing the value and necessity of harmonious marriages. In endeavouring, by way of contrast, to stress this main concern, he sometimes tends to develop the theme of marital misery to almost absurd extremes. This is certainly the case in *Der ungeliebte Mann* (1940) which is, without doubt, the strangest story the author ever wrote. Never did Fallada paint the miseries of an unhappy marriage in fuller details and in gloomier pictures. It is primarily the marriage of convenience which comes under the author's attack in this novel. The scene alternates between an estate in Prussia and a small provincial town. The owner of the estate is a blind widower, Siebenhaar, again a ruthless egotist, who has three young girls in his employ: Ilse Voß, Lola Bergfeld and Traute Kaiser, the youngest of the unhappy trio. Fritz Bleesern, the „ungeliebte Mann", is a misshapen little man who owns a hotel in the nearby town. Again Fallada presents a variation of the triangular plot, this time turning it about and exhibiting two men in love with a woman. All the characters in the book display a deep yearning for genuine love, yet none of them marry the person they really love. Ilse, although she is in love with another man, marries the „ungeliebte Mann", Fritz Bleesern, for the sake of convenience. Traute, too, loves another man, but, although initially she is determined to maintain „Sauberkeit, Ordnung, Klarheit", she marries blind Siebenhaar, partly out of a genuine feeling of compassion but chiefly because she has an eye on his property. Both unions, needless to say, soon develop into black marital discord. Siebenhaar turns out to be a selfish brute and a perfect despot in marriage. Traute soon finds herself no better than a slave, with her husband jealously guarding over her, even to the point where he has his estate protected from outside intrusions by a watchman and a vicious dog. All the women in the novel have an extremely weak opinion of man's ability to receive and give true love. Ilse speaks for all when she declares: „Vorher viel versprechen und hinterher gar nichts tun – so sind sie alle, alle!" And to her husband she says: „Ihr Männer habt einen komischen Begriff von der Liebe."[9] Hans Fallada here shows husband and wife engaged in a duel of the sexes which makes a happy relationship impossible and ends in frustration. All the characters finally fail to achieve „eine Gemeinsamkeit zweier Menschen, das beseligende Gefühl: du bist nie mehr mit nichts allein auf dieser Welt". Again Ilse speaks for all when she concludes: „Es wurde nichts Rechtes daraus, wenn man einen Mann ohne Liebe heiratete – sie hatte es erfahren, Traute hatte es erfahren, alle erfuhren es." [10] In this study of hatred in marriage Hans Fallada actually has nothing new to say on the old subject of the marriage of convenience. The conclusion is simply that marital calamity is due in every case to the lack of mutual affection and love. There can be no spiritual happiness in a relationship which lacks the *Hauptsache*, love, and which was originally founded on a deceitful contract. Fallada is convinced that as long as such motives are permitted to operate in the establishment of marriages, they are doomed to issue in tragedy for alle concerned.

Der ungeliebte Mann is a most unconvincing story. To make things even worse, Fallada concludes the novel with a „Nachspiel" entitled: „Die Verdammten und die Seligen", wherein he decides to separate the chaff from the wheat. By some miraculous turn of events the love of Fritz Bleesern, the „Ungeliebte, Verachtete, fast Verhaßte", finally succeeds in breaking through the „Eisenpanzer von Kälte" surrounding his wife's heart, thus securing at least one, not at all convincing, marital conciliation. Traute, who has fled the hell of her marriage to Siebenhaar, is duly compensated for the torture she has endured by being granted comfort in the embrace of

---

[9]   *Der ungeliebte Mann* (Berlin, Rowohlt Verlag, 1940), pp. 115, 162.
[10]   *Ibid.*, p. 165.

her old sweetheart, while Siebenhaar is damned to conclude his life in the company of Lola, a sensuous, scheming and loveless woman. If this novel illustrates anything at all, it is that Hans Fallada certainly is never at his best when depicting the miseries of marital life. In attempting to show the destructive consequences of unhappy marriages, he tends to exaggerate his portrayals, pushing the issues to untenable extremes and failing to define and develop the problems clearly, only finally to resolve them in a cheap and idyllic happy ending which minimises the power and influence of evil forces. *Der ungeliebte Mann,* which perhaps reflects to a certain extent the deterioration of Fallada's first marriage, is indeed a bad novel. It lacks a clear plot, narrative vigour and credible characterisation. But, happily, the book stands as an exception in our author's work.

In *Der Trinker* Fallada once again and for the last time depicted marital discord. The main problem here, even though it is often obscured by the ostensible theme indicated by the title of the novel, is doubtless the tragic breakup of a marriage. Fallada illustrates how the middle-aged, almost without either of the partners becoming fully aware of it, slowly but surely drift apart in marriage. Magda and Erwin Sommer were once a very happy couple. The early years of their union, with their struggles and successes achieved through mutual effort, had bound them closer together and the power of their love had always defied the hardships of many years of stress and strain. But then their love fails to endure. The middle-aged couple fails to overcome the perils of the critical years of their marriage. Both suffer from the weariness that comes from the saturation of a long union and both fail to weather the storm. And so their relationship withers into vague tactlessness and petty nagging:

Ich habe gesagt, daß Magda und ich uns an fast täglichen Streit gewöhnten. Freilich waren das eigentlich nur Quengeleien, kleine Sticheleien um ein Garnichts, etwas, das die zwischen uns immer wieder auftauchenden Spannungen ein wenig erleichterte. Auch das war eigentlich ein Wunder, aber kein schönes: viele Jahre hatten Magda und ich eine ausgesprochen gute Ehe geführt.

. . . .

Viele Jahre unserer Ehe waren wir immer wieder frisch verliebt ineinander.

. . . .

Erst, als unsere Streitereien begannen, merkte ich, wie fremd Magda und ich uns in den Jahren geworden waren, da sie ihre Hauswirtschaft besorgte und ich den Geschäften vorstand. [11]

How far apart they have indeed drifted and what stage of deterioration their marital union has reached, becomes evident when such a petty incident as the failure of the husband to wipe his shoes before entering the room suffices to set the stone in motion which finally turns into a disastrous avalanche. But this incident, of course, merely constitutes the straw that finally breaks the camel's back. And so the process of disintegration takes its fateful course. The husband seeks consolation in alcohol and a mercenary and intriguing woman, while the wife seeks and finds comfort in the love of another man. There are scenes describing bitter outbursts of hatred in this heartless story; scenes that find no parallels in any of Fallada's other books. And they are all the more tragic as they involve two people who had once been united in deep mutual love. The most vicious and heartbreaking of these incidents of antagonism occurs when the husband, who has become a drunkard and is living in sordid quarters, is caught redhanded by his wife while in the act of stealing valuables from his own home. In the ensuing tussle he threatens, in blind rage, to murder his wife – a threat which finally lands him in a mental institution:

Sie wendete den Kopf und sah mich an, lange. Ich merkte, wie sie erschrak, wie sie schnell atmete, sich zu sammeln versuchte.

„Erwin", sagte sie dann mit stockender Stimme, „Erwin! Wie siehst du aus!? . . . Erwin, denke daran, daß wir uns einmal liebgehabt haben!"

. . . .

Mich aber bewegten ganz andere Gefühle. Mit Zorn, mit Haß, mit Abneigung sah ich auf diese gepflegte, vom Schlaf gerötete Frau in ihrem seidenen blauen Schlafrock, ich, der aussah, als hätte ich mich in der Gosse gewälzt, ich, der stank wie ein Wiedehopf. Ich glaube, es muß die Mahnung an unsere Liebe von ehemals gewesen

[11] *Der Trinker,* pp. 9, 11.

sein, die mich in eine so sinnlose Wut versetzte. Ihre Worte, statt mich zu rühren, hatten mir nur den Abstand gegen das längst versunkene Damals fühlbar gemacht. Wir waren gleichgestellt, und da stand sie und hatte alles, und hier war ich, ein Kandidat des Nichts. Zornig stolperte ich auf Magda los ...

. . . .

Ich schüttelte die Fäuste nahe vor ihrem Gesicht.[12]

The intensity of the inner agony which Hans Fallada must have suffered while writing this semi-autobiographical novel is indeed difficult to estimate. In a very real sense this book crystallises Fallada's almost inhuman final despair. *Der Trinker* ends with the divorce of the couple and the permanent confinement of the husband in a mental institution.

It is noteworthy that in those of Fallada's novels which depict marital ordeals, the husband is in most cases made to bear the greater onus of the blame for the failure of a marriage. Fallada himself, incidentally, never hesitated to seek the blame for whatever misunderstandings occurred in his marriage in his own badly balanced and highly individualistic personality and to credit his wife with having at all times been responsible for the clearing up of these disagreements and the eventual marital adjustment:

Sie vergaß es auch in den dunkelsten Tagen nicht, daß wir zusammengehörten. Ich mochte noch so schwierig, noch so unleidlich sein, ich mochte mit allen Streit anfangen, wegen jeder Kleinigkeit wüten: sie bekam mich wieder zurecht. Einfach dadurch, daß sie da war. Daß ihre Güte, ihre Geduld, ihre Liebe über alles triumphierten. Daß sie unermüdlich wieder von vorn anfing, aufbaute, wo alles zerstört schien.[13]

It is also important to note that all the married couples which Fallada pictures involved in marital antagonisms have no children. Children are always suggested by the author as an absolutely essential ingredient of a truly fulfilled marriage. Children serve to bind husband and wife closer together and all happy couples in Fallada's work have at least one child, while those unions which fail to produce offspring inevitably end in misery. Magda

[12] *Ibid.*, p. 63.
[13] *Heute bei uns zu Haus*, p. 8.

and Erwin Sommer in *Der Trinker* were happy in the early years of their marriage. But, childless as their union has remained, they soon discover that in the later days of their marriage there proves to be no more mutual interest in life to hold them together. Both the women that love Johannes Gäntschow in *Wir hatten mal ein Kind* – the title of which is significant in itself – fail to bear him a living child which could have served as an important uniting link. Hans Fallada was himself extremely fond of children and in the chapter entiled „Porträt meiner Kinder" in *Heute bei uns zu Haus* we sense this feeling of affection when he writes:

In den „Geschichten aus der Murkelei" erzähle ich von einem Mann, der sich ein Dutzend Kinder wünschte, sechs Jungen und sechs Mädel. Er bekam aber nur zwei und mußte sich seine anderen Kinder träumen. Dieser Mann bin ich selbst, nur daß ich es immerhin auf drei Kinder gebracht habe, zwei Jungen und ein Mädel ...

Schon als ich noch jung war, als ich überhaupt noch nicht an das Heiraten dachte, schienen mir Kinder der einzig wirklich erstrebenswerte Reichtum.

. . . .

Kinder sind Reichtum, weil man Kindern immer schenken kann, und nur der ist reich, der täglich schenken kann.

. . . .

Ich habe es schon erzählt: als der Uli geboren wurde, ging es knapp bei uns zu, wir hatten ziemlich viel Sorgen. Aber es war eine Wonne, es war ein vollkommen neues Land, das Suse und ich entdeckten, und alle Sorgen wogen federleicht gegen diese Entdeckerfreude. [14]

Reading these lines one cannot but be reminded of the joy and light which their „Murkel" brings into the dismal existence of the Pinnebergs in *Kleiner Mann – was nun?*.

It is now time to turn our attention to those of our author's novels which deal with marital concord or in which marital problems are solved and love finally triumphs.

It was in *Kleiner Mann – was nun?* that Hans Fallada for the first time described in moving terms the joy and harmony of blissful marriage. It was here that he elevated the theme of matrimony to a truly artistic level. No other novel of our author sets forth so fully and with such deep insight the happy marital life

[14] *Ibid.*, pp. 222–223.

of his „little man". It is in this book also that Fallada portrayed his most lovable female character, Lämmchen, presenting in her the classical personification of his many loving and characterful women and endowing her with all their best faculties. The portrait of Lämmchen rises, indeed, to the level of an ageless ideal of womanly loyalty and conjugal love.

In *Kleiner Mann – was nun?* Hans Fallada presents a conception of marital bliss, undisturbed by any serious marital problems, which may, to be sure, provoke the criticism of some readers. It will always be argued by the sceptics that Fallada's view in this book is too simple and idyllic to merit serious consideration. To argue in this manner is to misunderstand the author's main intention. For Fallada was here not intent on analysing marital problems and proposing solutions to them. He seeks solely to present a timeless portrait of what a truly happy marriage can be like and, more specifically, to point to the importance of such a union in the social life of his „little man". Above all he also wants to emphasise the significant function of the woman within the marital union. In *Kleiner Mann – was nun?* we see how Pinneberg's marriage succeeds in breaking through the isolation of the „little man" and, in times of utmost need and disillusionment, provides him with a last refuge to which he may flee from the struggles of a society whose problems he can no longer come to grips with:

Lämmchen wollte ihren Jungen nur ein Weilchen im Arm halten, draußen war ja die wilde weite Welt mit viel Radau und Feindschaft, die gar nichts Gutes von einem wußte und wollte – war es da nicht gut, wenn eines am anderen lag und sich fühlte wie ein kleine warme Insel? [15]

No doubt a scene such as this one can be taken as an example of Fallada's tendency to idealise and simplify the issues and to come precariously close to permitting his account to deteriorate into a naive idyllicism. But there is, obviously, more to it than that. It expresses, above all, a search for human communion and certain inviolate values that fulfil man's very real need to be lifted

---

[15]   *Kleiner Mann – was nun?*, p. 162.

above the din of „die wilde weite Welt". This is far removed from
any form of escapism. *Kleiner Mann – was nun?* reveals our
author's deep understanding of the profound forces that unite two
loving people and constitute an indestructible bulwark against
all adversities. It is the strength of the bond uniting man and
wife in a happy union which is able to mitigate the stress of
the little family's existence and enables them to preserve a certain
degree of self-respect and honesty. Such simple words as: „Aber
du kannst mich doch ansehen! Immer und immer! Du bist doch
bei mir, wir sind doch beisammen . . .",[16] charged, as they are,
with deep love and expressing, as they do, all that really matters
in a harmonious marriage, give the „little man" the strength
he requires to bear his lot. Mutual trust and love, then, are the
forces which stem the tide of disillusionment and despair that
threatens to wash Fallada's „little man" out into the desolate
sea of total human degradation. And it is, above all, the love
of the woman, her sustaining spirit and innate sense of values,
which tips the scales and aids the „little man" in the struggle
that finally leads to a victorious breakthrough. When Pinneberg,
brought down to utter poverty and despair, declares his willingness
to steal some wood, it is his wife who resolutely refuses to permit
him to slide into crime, even of the pettiest kind. She demonstrates
her determination to maintain, through her love, the moral integrity of her husband when she says to Jachmann:

„Er soll nicht runter, Jachmann, er soll nicht! Das soll er behalten.
Luxus – ja, vielleicht, aber das ist unser einziger Luxus, den halt
ich fest, da passiert nichts, Jachmann." . . . „Sehen Sie mal den Murkel
in seinem Bettchen, und nun kommt es vielleicht wieder besser und
der Junge rappelt sich wieder auf und hat eine Stellung und eine
Arbeit, die ihm Spaß macht, und verdient wieder Geld. Und da soll
er immer denken: das hast du gemacht und so bist du gewesen. Es
ist nicht das Holz, Jachmann, es sind nicht die Gesetze – . . ." „Aber
der Junge kann's nicht", sagt Lämmchen eifrig. „Der ist wie sein
Vater, . . . Und darum ist es kein Luxus, Jachmann, das muß er
behalten, und wenn er jetzt manchmal denkt, er kann sein, wie die
andern: er kann nicht. Er muß sauber bleiben. Und dafür passe ich

[16] *Ibid.*, p. 353.

auf, Jachmann, deswegen nimmt er keine Stellung wieder an, die auf Schwindel aufgebaut ist." [17]

And this, indeed, is exactly what Lämmchen does. She sets herself to keep her husband clean, and in the end she succeeds. The guiding and strong hand of the woman stretches out to save the man from the swamp that threatens to drown him. No other female figure in Fallada's work measures up fully to the stature of Lämmchen, and no other woman performs more adequately the function of being the guardian of society's lasting values. Here, indeed, woman is once again viewed as the very buttress of society.

Pinneberg, in contrast to men like Johannes Gäntschow or Karl Siebrecht, finds bliss in his marriage with Lämmchen by accepting the domination of the loving and strong-willed woman. And so in the end love prevails and the Pinnebergs, inspite of everything, maintain their sense of values and a strong belief in the essential goodness of life. Uplifted by the reassuring influence of his wife, the weak-willed „little man" finally struggles through to his „Dennoch" and returns to his Lämmchen, the very foundation of his existence. It was all of this that prompted Carl Zuckmayer to laud Fallada's novel in the following terms:

... daß die Liebe und die Tapferkeit und die Herzenswärme zweier Menschen stärker ist als ihre Not – daß etwas bleibt und triumphiert, was nicht zu ersticken ist – ... Das ist das Wunderbare an dem Buch: es schenkt unmerklich, und ohne daß man die Gebärde des Schenkens gewahr wird, das Notwendigste, das Seltenste, das Menschlichste, was es auf der Erde gibt: Vertrauen. [18]

Here Zuckmayer touches upon one of Fallada's truly great gifts, his ability to fathom the depths of man's most fundamental emotions in a manner that is so unassuming that it almost escapes our attention. Never again did Hans Fallada sing the praise of what is best in married life, of marital concord and the love and strength of woman in such tenderly constrained yet forceful tones as he did in *Kleiner Mann – was nun?*

Already in *Bauern, Bonzen und Bomben* Hans Fallada had

[17] *Ibid.*, pp. 348–349.
[18] Carl Zuckmayer, „Ein Buch (Fallada: *Kleiner Mann – was nun?)*", *Die Literatur*, (1932/33), 100.

briefly introduced the theme of the relations of man and wife and, in the figure of Elise Tredup, the „little man's" courageous wife, presented his first interpretation of the loving and strong-minded woman. Here already marriage is seen as the last support of the „little man" and as the only means of overcoming his social and spiritual loneliness. When in the end all imaginable misfortunes befall the unfortunate little newspaper reporter, Max Tredup, and he stands alone in utter despondency, forsaken and accused by all, it is his wife who remains as the only source of encouragement:

Aber noch immer wagt Tredup nicht hochzusehen, er fühlt, es ist zu Ende mit ihm ... – er kommt nicht wieder hoch.
　　Er sieht doch auf ... er muß aufsehen. Der Blick seiner Frau trifft ihn: Elise lächelt. Sie lächelt ihm zu mit den Augen, Mut machend, ich verlaß dich nicht. [19]

There is little doubt that, had her husband not been murdered, Elise, like Lämmchen, would have succeeded in providing him with the strength to hold out and to make a new start.

　　We might mention at this point that in *Wer einmal aus dem Blechnapf frißt* the tragic fate of the „little man", Willi Kufalt, is further aggravated by the fact that, upon his reentry into society, the ex-convict fails to meet a suitable mate who could have aided him in acquitting himself of the task of rehabilitation in society. For it is surely conceivable that, had Willi Kufalt been blessed with the good fortune of finding and growing to love a woman of the calibre of a Lämmchen or Elise Tredup, the tragic end might well have been averted. Kufalt does meet a woman and even gets engaged to her. The few weeks of his engagement to Hildegard do, in fact, turn out to be the happiest and most successful of his short stay in the world outside. But the bliss turns out to be short-lived; for his relationship to Hildegard lacks the essential elements needed to built a successfull marriage. It lacks the mutual trust and unconditional confidence in each other required of the partners of such a union, and it lacks, above all, what was always for Fallada the *sine qua non:* the sustaining

[19]　*Bauern, Bonzen und Bomben*, p. 461.

influence of a steadfast woman. Hildegard Harder is in want of
the inner stability and the dignity of a Lämmchen, qualities which
could have been a source of strength for Kufalt. Hildegard fails
to win Kufalt's full confidence, the result being that at no time
does he feel obliged to reveal to her the full truth about his
background, thus building his relationship to her on a shaky
foundation from the very outset. And so when in the end the
truth of Kufalt's past finally comes to light and the ex-convict,
falsely accused of a theft, stands in dire need of an understanding
and trusting heart, Hildegard fails miserably to stretch out a helping
hand, and we hear no more of her.

In *Wolf unter Wölfen* Hans Fallada once again returned to
the theme of the function of the woman in society and showed
her as its very essence. Petra Ledig, the girl from the streets with
whom the ex-lieutenant, Wolfgang Pagel, is living, is again a
being imbued with all the rare qualities of a Lämmchen. Young
Pagel, who has been unemployed for months and has been paying
his way by gambling gains, abandons Petra after a series of
fateful misunderstandings on the very day he had promised to
marry her. He leaves Berlin and seeks relief in the country where
he gets employment on a manorial estate. But in this case Fallada's
usually firm belief in the therapeutic powers inherent in a rustic
environment, a problem that will concern us in our next chapter,
proves to be illusory. Pagel fails to absorb the hoped-for regenerative forces from his close contact with the soil and nature. In the
end, it is the image of Petra alone which saves him from utter
disillusionment, and it is her love that leads him on towards a
new life. Wolfgang Pagel, too, like Pinneberg in *Kleiner Mann –
was nun?*, returns to the woman who has never ceased to love
him and is not ashamed to recognise her as the one remaining
stabilising influence. Petra Ledig has that aquilibrium of the soul
and displays that unconditional intuitive trust both in herself and
her fellow beings which makes her almost a Kleistian figure. At
a critical juncture of her relationship to Wolfgang she had firmly
told him: „Daß ich trau!" [20] It is this deep-rooted confidence in

[20] *Wolf unter Wölfen*, I, 64.

her loved one which upholds her throughout her darkest hours. In the end it is Petra's qualities of understanding, her love and, above all her faith which remain victorious. The love of woman reigns supreme:

Es ist kein Glück, das von äußeren Dingen abhängig ist, es ruht in ihr, wie der Kern in der Nuß. Eine Frau, die liebt und sich geliebt weiß, kennt das Glück, das immer bei ihr ist, wie ein seliges Geflüster im Ohr – den Lärm des Tages übertönend. Eine liebende Geliebte ist das ruhige Glück, dem nichts mehr zu wünschen bleibt.[21]

In *Kleiner Mann – großer Mann, alles vertauscht* Hans Fallada again interprets the marital life of his „little man" and in the figure of Karla Schreyvogel presents yet another version of the resolute and loving woman. The Schreyvogel family is in fact a re-embodiment of the Pinneberg family. We have already mentioned in our preceding chapter how in *Kleiner Man – großer Man, alles vertauscht* the possession of money threatens to disrupt the happy marriage of the „little man", thus destroying his last refuge. Max Schreyvogel proves incapable of drawing any lasting gains from his newly-acquired wealth. He becomes a detestable loafer and a drunkard, who remains insensitive to the pleadings of his lovable wife. Again Fallada utilises the triangular plot to develop the theme of the alienation of man and wife. The forbidden fruit in this case is Leonore, the seductive daughter of the owner of the neighbouring manorial estate. Bored as Max is in his new role as a millionaire, he soon falls an easy prey to the allurements of this shallow and scheming girl, in whose company he henceforth wastes his money. Inevitably, husband and wife drift apart. But once again it is the strong-willed woman who refuses to let things deteriorate to the point of no return. Karla demonstrates her determination to uphold her marriage when, at the most critical stage of her crumbling relationship to Max, she resolutely tells him: „Nur, Max, ich warne dich: ich bin geduldig, aber alles lasse ich mir nicht kaputt machen, meine Ehe nicht und dich nicht!"[22] And when her husband fails to

---

[21] *Ibid.*, II. 1156.
[22] *Kleiner Mann – großer Mann, alles vertauscht*, p. 215.

take this warning to heart, Karla soon shows in a tangible way that she meant every word she said. Max, who has become an alcoholic, awakens one morning to find himself imprisoned in the little garden-house of the estate. During his confinement, which lasts for months, Karla refuses to see him. She takes the reins firmly into her hands and sets to work to rid herself of the wealth that has been the source of her unhappiness. In contrast to her husband, she puts the money to a meaningful use by building new homes for the poor in the nearby community, a project which finally exhausts all her funds, thus achieving her main purpose. Max has in the meantime regained his mental and physical health and a marital conciliation is finally achieved. Love in the end gains the day, and once again Fallada shows the woman as the party responsible for the preservation of society's lasting values. Karla Schreyvogel, who had always professed her firm belief in „Anstand", „Ehrlichkeit", and „Freundschaft", demonstrates her determination and ability to uphold and maintain these values, and in the end her husband has to admit: „Sie war stärker als ich, aber ich hoffte, daß auch ich einmal stärker werden würde – als ich jetzt war." [23]

At one point Max Schreyvogel, recalling how he had betrayed his wife by revealing their most intimate marital problems to Leonore, ruefully exclaims:

Ich schäme mich noch heute wie ich . . . Stück für Stück unserer Ehe vor diesem kalten, berechnenden Mädchen bloßlegte. Denn die Dinge einer wirklichen Ehe sind so, daß sie ein Bloßstellen vor Fremden nicht vertragen. Schon die leiseste, nur in einem Ton liegende Anklage gegen den Ehepartner, vor einem Fremden geäußert, verletzt die Ehe. Ehe ist immer ein wahrhaftes Geheimnis zu zweien, ein echtes „Tabu" – wenn sie nämlich eine Ehe ist. [24]

Again and again Hans Fallada demonstrates his deep conviction that the relations of man and wife must be such as to constitute „ein wahrhaftes Geheimnis zu zweien" if they are to issue in a truly fulfilled marriage. Whenever this „Tabu" is not honoured, the bond of matrimony crumbles.

[23] *Ibid.*, p. 385.
[24] *Ibid.*, p. 299.

Der eiserne Gustav is a family portrait wherein Hans Fallada's prime concern is not the relations of husband and wife. He deals here with other important family relationships. It is, above all, the *Generationsproblem* on which he attempts to shed some light. We have already mentioned that this voluminous novel is an account of the decay of a lower-middle class family. It is first and foremost the struggle between generations which brings about the decline of the significant social unit of the family which at one point is referred to as „der Grundpfeiler vom Staat". Fallada in this book places the main blame on the older generation. It is the uncomprehending attitudes adopted by the parents, and particularly by the father, that breed an atmosphere of intense hostility in the family. *Der eiserne Gustav* is Fallada's most extreme artistic restatement of the father-children and, above all, the father-son conflict, which, as stated earlier, was one of the most painful and crucial experiences of his own life. The threatening figure of the father dominates the whole Hackendahl family; the father represents „Befehl, Urteil, strengstes Gericht". The *Generationsproblem,* and particularly the conflict between father and son, was a problem that was obviously too intimately linked with the author's own life to permit a truly meaningful depiction in a sublimated form. *Der eiserne Gustav* is in fact the only book in which it is dwelled upon at length. Fallada did, however, return to the problem – in most cases briefly – in some of his other novels. In *Der Jungherr von Strammin* (1943), a novel which first appeared, in 1943, in a shortened form in the paper „Die Welt", then was printed twice more in serial form in the „Morgenpost" (November 20, 1952 – February 8, 1953) and in the „Hamburger Abendblatt" (December 25, 1955 – January 27, 1956) and was finally published in book form in 1965 under the title *Junger Herr – ganz groß,* our author shows father and son drifting apart to the point where the father finally rids himself of his son for good. It is not the main character, Lutz von Strammin, whose relations with his parents are also somewhat strained, but rather his wayward uncle, Gregor von Lassenthin, who is shown in an irreconcilable discord with his father. In this story, which describes the often rather unlikely escapades of a young aristocrat who goes out into the world to prove himself, Hans Fallada for the first and only time gave a sympathetic portrayal of a father and placed the full blame for the disruption of the father-son relationship squarely on the shoulders of the son. Gregor von Lassenthin is an irresponsible, debauched loafer who brings nothing but heartache into the life of his widowed father. The old Lassenthin is, to be sure, a strange enough *Kauz*, a completely ostracised „Rauhbold", as he is commonly called in the area of his estate. Yet his frightening behaviour and all his eccentricities turn out to be but a mask concealing what is basically a kindhearted and very lonely human being. He proves this when, after having bought his freedom from Gregor, he adopts his son's illegitimate son and starts a new life devoted to the education of this „Erbprinzen". Lutz von Strammin's father, too, is credited in the story with understanding and foresight when, at a crucial juncture, he sides with his son against the mother, who tries to nullify Lutz's determination to undertake a rather dangerous journey in search of Gregor, not realising that she is in fact attempting to frustrate her son's firm resolve to prove himself as an independent and mature man. It is obvious from this book that Fallada did not view his own conflict with his father from a one-sided standpoint. As late as 1947 our author returned to deal with the problem of the father-son conflict. It is in but a brief yet extremely effective scene in *Jeder stirbt für sich allein* that Fallada describes the bitter confrontation between the boy, Kuno-Dieter, who has fled from his criminal parents and has been adopted by a warmhearted elderly couple, and his degraded father. Here it is the son who completely disavows his father with the heart-rending cry „Ich hab keinen Vater!" and then sets out to build a new life for himself under a new name. Fallada's portrayal of the father-son conflict seems to have been governed by a painful realisation that this tragic struggle is almost inevitable and does not lend itself to a harmonious solution.

To return to *Der eiserne Gustav:* Fallada here depicts not only the violent struggle of the children against parental authority. He shows also how brothers and sisters, too, drift apart, thus leaving the family in a sorry state of total fragmentation. The following

scene between mother Hackendahl and her daughters may serve
as an illustration of the family's pitiful state of disunion:

> Aber, Mutter, rief Sophie entsetzt, hinter Vaters Rücken darfst du
> Erich doch kein Geld geben. Ihr müßt doch zusammenhalten als
> Eltern, ihr seid doch ein Ehepaar ... Wenn ich solchen Quatsch bloß
> höre! sagte Eva verächtlich ...
>
> . . . .
>
> Und ich mache es nicht mehr mit! rief Sophie entschlossen ... Heute
> noch spreche ich mit der Frau Oberin und heute abend ziehe ich
> mit Sack und Pack in das Mutterhaus!
> Sophie! rief die Mutter flehend. Tu bloß das nicht! Vater erlaubt es
> nie. Du bist doch unsere Tochter, und wir sind eine Familie und
> gehören zusammen ...
> Jawohl, zum Streiten gehören wir zusammen! sagte Eva zornig.
> Sophie hat ganz recht, sie soll machen, daß sie wegkommt! Und
> ich gehe auch bald. Jeder muß sehen, wo er bleibt, und das mit
> Familie und Elternliebe und Geschwistern – das ist alles Unsinn!
> Aber, Evchen, sage doch das nicht! Wir lieben uns doch untereinander.
> Gar nicht lieben wir uns! rief Eva trotzig. Nicht ausstehen können
> wir uns ... [25]

The only gleam of light in this book is the relationship between
Otto, the quiet and weak-willed eldest son, and his hunchbacked
little wife, Gertrud, a relationship which had been maintained as
an illegitimate union for many years. Here again Fallada returns
to depict the joys of a happy marriage, and in the figure of
Gertrud portrays yet another of his women of strong character.
It is again the love of the woman which upholds the „Gemeinsamkeit, leidgehärtet in einer Zeit, da fast alles zerfiel", and again
this „Gemeinsamkeit" is seen as the „little man's" last haven into
which he can escape from the perils of a time that is terribly out
of joint: „Ach, die beiden im Leben zu kurz Gekommenen, er
mit dem schwachen Willen, sie mit dem verkrüppelten Körper –
hier zu zweien, nein, zu dreien, in Küche und Stube, allein für
sich, geben und empfangen sie so viel Glück!" [26] Even after
Otto's death on the battlefields of the First World War, Gertrud
remains the loving woman she had always been, bringing that

---

[25] *Der eiserne Gustav*, pp. 26–27.
[26] *Ibid.*, p. 75.

solace to her fellow beings which true love alone can offer. She
is the only one who offers her comforting heart to her destitute
sister-in-law, Eva Hackendahl, who has lapsed into prostitution
and utter moral corruption:

> ... eine Frau, der die Liebe heilig ist, wird stets der grollen, die aus
> den Liebesäußerungen ein Gewerbe macht ... Und doch läßt Tutti
> Hackendahl immer noch die Schwägerin in die Wohnung, erträgt sie,
> duldet sie, läßt sie sich aussprechen ... Weil nämlich Gertrud Hacken-
> dahl versteht, daß jeder Mensch im Elend eine Insel haben muß, zu
> der er fliehen kann aus der Trostlosigkeit des Alltags, daß er eine
> Stätte der Geduld wissen muß, etwas wie eine Heimat ... Sie ist
> solche Heimat für Eva ... [27]

It is as „eine Stätte der Geduld" that Hans Fallada time and
again portrayed his most prominent female characters. Here,
indeed, Gertrud Hackendahl, once again, like Elise Tredup,
Lämmchen, Petra Ledig and Karla Schreyvogel, represents, in the
words of H. A. Wyk mentioned before, „the return of the tender
and all-bountiful love of woman". And these women are not mere
types. Their personalities are always highly individualised and
their characterisation vivid and convincing. What they all have in
common are their rare qualities of understanding, their trust and
patience, and, above all else, their redeeming love.

The fairy tale *Märchen vom Stadtschreiber, der aufs Land flog,*
which the author in its preface dedicates to E. T. A. Hoffmann
and calls a „Zaubergeschichte aus dunklen Mächten und Liebe
entstanden", again introduces love as one of its main themes.
The story, which, as we have mentioned, Harry Slochower has
very convincingly shown to be in fact a brilliant satire on
Nazidom, is somewhat reminiscent in its theme of Kafka's
Die Verwandlung. In contrast to Gregor's sorry lot in Kafka's
gruesome tale, however, it is the power of love alone which in
the end succeeds in overcoming all the adversities facing the
transformed „little man" and which finally brings about the
ultimate and lasting reconversion of Guntram Spatt into an
autonomous and proud human being. And again it is the love
of woman, that of his cousin, Monika, which breaks the spell:

[27] *Ibid.,* p. 323.

„Schien es ihm doch fast schmachvoll, daß er so lange als niedriger Spatz bei ihr gelebt, von ihr abhängig und ihr untertan und am Ende allein durch ihre Liebestränen zum Leben wiedererweckt." (sic) [28] This allegorical tale touches upon nearly all of Fallada's main themes but it celebrates, above all, the transforming power of womanly love.

The autobiographical elements in *Der Alpdruck* are indubitable. The story of the morphinist author Dr. Doll and his wife, Alma, represents an artistic recreation of many of Fallada's own experiences following the collapse of the Third Reich. As we mentioned earlier, Fallada portrayed his second wife in the figure of Alma Doll. Again, as in *Ein Mann will hinauf,* the problem of second marriage is not developed by the author. In stark contrast to his personal experiences, Fallada in *Der Alpdruck* depicts no conflicts which may follow upon remarriage, and only at one point does the memory of Dr. Doll's former wife crop up as a disuniting factor. Doll's alliance with Alma is a happy one, welded together in times of utmost need. In the figure of Alma, Hans Fallada again portrayed one of his loving female characters, the light of the home and the comfort of her husband. She, too, has become addicted to the use of narcotics which permits her to escape from the pressures of the times. But in the end she succeeds in restoring herself and her husband to the „Einklang mit sich selbst". Tenderly Doll calls his wife „meine große Verwöhnerin", and again Hans Fallada shows marriage as the only means of overcoming the bitter loneliness of the individual:

Oh, das Glück, wieder beieinander zu sein, zu fühlen, wo man hingehört in dieser eisigen Welt von Vereinsamung und Zerstörung... Zu hören, wie sie ihn voll Stolz der Zimmergenossin vorstellt: „Das ist mein Mann!" Und er weiß doch, er ist bloß ein alt gewordener Mann in einem zerknitterten, gar nich einwandfreien Sommeranzug, er selber auch zerknittert und ganz und gar nicht einwandfrei aussehend. Aber das alles sieht sie nicht, weil sie ihn eben liebt, sie ist blind dafür. [29]

[28] *Märchen vom Stadtschreiber, der aufs Land flog* (Berlin, Rowohlt Verlag, 1935), p. 224.
[29] *Der Alpdruck* (Berlin, Aufbau-Verlag, 1947), p. 141.

Fallada's second wife, as Jürgen Manthey has pointed out, did in fact love him in her own somewhat naive yet nevertheless devoted way. Strengthened no doubt by their mutual problem of alcoholism and drug addiction, she showed a feeling of strong attachment to and deep affection for her critically ill husband right to the tragic end of his life.

In *Jeder stribt für sich allein* Fallada for the last time exhibited the marital life of his „little man". In contrast to Erwin and Magda Sommer in *Der Trinker,* who failed to weather the perils of middle-age, Otto and Anna Quangel are drawn even closer together in the later days of their marriage. Bereaved by the death of their only son, this middle-aged couple decide to do what little they can to resist the „Machtapparat" of the Hitler regime. Their mutual struggle provides them with a new purpose in life, binding them ever closer together and engendering in their minds that deep joy which springs from the assurance of an inner spiritual communion of two loving souls: „Sie arbeiteten in der schönsten Gemeinsamkeit, und diese tiefe, innere Gemeinsamkeit, die sie nach so langer Ehe jetzt erst kennenlernten, wurde ihnen zu einem großen Glück."[30] When the couple is finally arrested and imprisoned, it is the certainty of their mutual love which enables them, even in separation, to endure the tortures inflicted upon them and to hold out to the bitter end. Here the spiritual bond that unites man and wife proves stronger than all adversities and endures even in the face of death.

Few authors have demonstrated the kind of deep insight into the nature of the relations of man and wife as that displayed by Hans Fallada throughout his work. If it were for nothing else, his books would still have great value indeed as truly enlightened interpretations of these important relations. They would also be of value for the unique position assigned in them to the role of women in society. Fully emancipated, Hans Fallada's women stand, not as a means for the satisfaction of the desires and wants of man, but as an end in themselves and as the very salvation of

---

[30] *Jeden stirbt für sich allein,* p. 166.

man. The love of woman moulds the character of man and uplifts his spirits in times of crises.

We have shown, we believe, that it would be unjust to contend that Fallada's presentation of the themes of love and marriage is too unproblematical to deserve serious consideration. Seldom has an author been so fully aware of all the intricate problems that have to be coped with in the partnership of husband and wife. Only once, in fact, did our author write a pure and uncomplicated love story in his delightful novel *Zwei zarte Lämmchen – weiß wie Schnee* (1953) in which he describes the amusing and moving courtship of two young white-collar workers. The one element, however, that all of Hans Fallada's works have in common is the author's unwavering determination to proclaim and celebrate the all-redeeming power of human love. As he puts it in those simple yet significant words with which he concludes his *Märchen vom Stadtschreiber, der aufs Land flog:* „Was brauchet der Mensch denn Flügel – hat er doch die Liebe!"

III

THE RETURN TO THE SOIL

There is doubtless some justification in contending that the „return to nature" cry is one to which the German seems to have always lent a particularly sympathetic ear. The yearning for *Natur* has for the German the connotation of a variety of emotional experiences. These experiences are often formulated by such terms as *Mutter Erde, Heimat, Herkunft* and can probably never be fully understood in all their far-reaching implications by the outsider. What to the foreigner may well seem sentimental or even reactionary is more often than not to the German a very genuine and essentially positive attitude. Basically this attitude represents, on the one hand, an attempt to become aware again of traditions and national cultural values which seem to be disappearing in a hostile industrialised environment, and, on the other, a search for forces which, it is assumed, will aid in restoring a disrupted spiritual equilibrium. The disturbance of man's mental balance may be caused by social and economic crises such as war, inflation, unemployment, or the like. More often, however, it is life in an inorganic society and particularly in the modern industrialised city which is believed to exert a damaging and corrupting influence on the individual's spiritual life and which, for the sake of his salvation, necessitates an escape to a more „natural" and stable life in the country. Ultimately, this is an attitude that represents a genuine and earnest attempt to seek assurance of the continuing existence of certain immutable values. The juxtaposition of what is considered to be a more or less decadent and artificial life in the modern city and a healthy rustic life is, of course, not a theme peculiar to German literature. It is, nevertheless, a motif that has been a favourite with many German writers and a term such as *Heimatkunst* or the corrupt slogan *Blut und Boden* immediately spring to mind. The cultural and social criticism implied in this whole complex of attitudes is apparent.

Hans Fallada, too, introduced the contrast between city and country life and the flight from the former to the latter as one of his major themes in many of his novels. It will be our task in this chapter to determine to what extent this contrast does in fact entail an implicit or explicit criticism of modern society and its values and to what degree the return to the soil succeeds in producing the hoped-for regeneration in our author's characters. In this connection, we shall attempt to show that Hans Fallada never relied exclusively on what Harry Slochower has termed his „agrarian talisman".[1] He was far indeed from glorifying every aspect of life in a rural community and rigourously avoided a mere black and white presentation of the contrast between life in the country, on the one hand, and urban living on the other. Consequently it will become apparent that, contrary to the views expressed by some critics of Fallada's work, our author's novels can hardly be regarded as having been in tune with any fixed ideology such as, for instance, that preached by the „blood and soil" philosophy.

Hans Fallada was himself well acquainted with both country and city life. He was born in the little university town of Greifswald and his boyhood memories are of excursions into the countryside and to the sea, where he stood on a dune gazing into the distance over the water and suddenly becoming intensely aware of his existence as an integral part of a great and well-wrought universe. After an extremely difficult and tragic youth that was marked by frequent severe illnesses, confinements in sanatoriums, attempted suicides, a fatal duel with a close friend and the already mentioned constant tensions with his parents, especially his father, the hypersensitive Fallada left his home at an early age to live in the country where he became familiar with the elements of agriculture and held various positions on the great

[1] Harry Slochower, *op. cit.*, 24.

manorial estates of East Prussia. Later he moved to the cities and spent considerable time in both small and great urban centres, notably Berlin, earning his livelihood by working in a great variety of capacities. Deep in his heart, however, he always remained loyal to his intense love for nature and life in the country. H. A. Wyk has recounted a conversation he had with Hans Fallada in Berlin:

Fallada asks himself what is the matter with this stone-bound city of Berlin and its literary business, „Everything is reduced to pulp in talk, everything is put on paper, so that in the end one has the feeling that life itself cannot be found." ... Fallada refers to the life of peasants and charcoal-burners, who are rarely familiar with books but who know how to live better than people can in this hideous machine of a city. „I want to write books and live in the country ... My great dream is to have a little peasant holding." [2]

This great dream of his became reality when the success of *Kleiner Mann – was nun?* provided him with the means to purchase a little farm in Mecklenburg. Recounting how his wife persuaded him to invest his money in this manner, he writes in one of his autobiographical novels: „Sie fasste mich bei meiner Liebe zum Landleben, ich war viele Jahre meines Lebens Landwirt gewesen. Sie erzählte mir von einem Haus auf dem Lande, von einem Garten, vom Vieh, vom Wasser, an dem wir wohnen würden." [3] And so Fallada returned to the country and wrote his books surrounded by plants and animals, water and the open countryside. His little farm became his retreat from the hurried bustle of the great city of Berlin and quite categorically he declares: „ – Berlin? Ach was, Berlin! Mahlendorf ! ! !" [4] It may be assumed, then, that it was in Mahlendorf that his search for „life itself" was to meet with greater success and his view to be less obstructed than in the „hideous machine" of the city of Berlin.

We shall attempt to determine, first, to what degree Fallada's move into the country and his permanent rooting in the soil did in fact succeed in engendering the sought-for revitalisation of his

[2] H. A. Wyk, *op. cit.,* 330–331.
[3] *Heute bei uns zu Haus,* p. 35.
[4] *Ibid.,* p. 50.

spirits and what positive effects it may have had particularly on his artistic activities. Then we shall investigate how contact with the soil affects the characters in his books and to what extent agrarian living as an alternative to urban existence is in fact regarded by the author as being the source of salutary and rejuvinating forces.

Heute bei uns zu Haus deals at great length with the author's own life on his little holding in the country. We are not only given a vivid and humorous account of his daily activities on the farm but are also permitted a glance into his study and are told something about his creative process. On numerous occasions, however, we cannot fail to wonder just how beneficial the rustic way of living proves itself to be, especially for the pursuits of an artist, and to query wherein its advantages over life in the city do in fact lie. For it is surely not easy to see how, for instance, the incessant bellowing of a hungry cow accompanying every line the author puts on paper – („. . . sie brüllt immer weiter, jede Zeile mindestens zweimal!") – constitutes a more soothing or invigorating experience than, say, the honking of motorcar-horns outside a city-apartment window. And when this same cow and details of the torturous hunger-cure it is undergoing, provide the material for one whole chapter, (written in a room resounding with „Olsch's" constant protestations), we may indeed begin to question the effectiveness of the restorative or stimulating qualities supposedly inherent in country life. Nor, it would seem, do the frequent interruptions of the author's creative work in the form of perilous excursions into shaky treetops in pursuit of his swarming bees, provide him with interludes of the kind one would like to consider conducive to the restoring of mental equilibrium. Distractions such as these are, to say the least, surely as time-consuming and annoying and probably as destructive to intellectual and artistic pursuits as any that may accompany life in the city. And Hans Fallada shows himself to be fully aware of this fact, for he repeatedly pokes open fun at his rather comical situation:

„Gott, wie siehst du aus!" rief Suse. „Die haben dich ja schön vorgehabt! Hast du wenigstens den Schwarm?" „Jawohl, ich habe

ihn", sage ich traurig und schleiche mich zu meiner Schreiberei. Es dauert eine ganze Zeit, bis ich mit ihr in Gang komme. Mein Gesicht ist in einem scheußlichen Zustand. Langsam konzentriere ich meine Gedanken wieder auf die Arbeit, ich fange an zu schreiben ...
Ich habe noch nicht lange geschrieben, da klopft es an meiner Tür. „Na, was ist denn nun wieder los?!" rufe ich sehr ungnädig. „Lieber Junge", sagt Suse sehr vorsichtig, „ich fürchte, dein Schwarm ist wieder ausgerissen. Er sitzt wieder oben im Baum ..."

. . . .

Nach drei Minuten lege ich den Halter aus der Hand. [5]

Is Hans Fallada, we may ask, perhaps cautiously satirising a mode of living which, at the time of his writing, was believed to provide the fool-proof remedy for all the ills of modern civilisation? Considering the author's strong anti-Nazi feelings, it would seem reasonable to assume that he was at least attempting to intimate that he did not consider the „natural" way of life as the panacea for all evils of modernism. Fallada's love for rustic life and farming certainly had no political roots and cannot be regarded in any way to have been of the kind that could be utilised for political propaganda purposes. We shall see later how this view may be substantiated by evidence from some of his other novels. But in *Heute bei uns zu Haus,* too, there are other definite indications which point in this direction and make the author's position perfectly clear. Thus, for instance, Fallada expresses great delight at his ownership of a new automobile, the very symbol of technological progress and mechanisation, and devotes a whole chapter of the book to his „Glück aus Leder, Lack und Stahl". And in the last chapter, sober reflections lead him to bid farewell to his little farm because the education of his children necessitates a move to the vicinity of a city, thus clearly indicating that the author was well aware of the lack in the country of many essential elements of cultural living.

Fallada's account of his literary activities in *Heute bei uns zu Haus* again makes no specific mention of any aspects of his life in the country which may in any way be regarded as having exerted

[5] *Ibid.,* pp. 127–128.

a stimulating or revitalising influence on his creative and imaginative faculties. We have already mentioned some of the interruptions which can hardly be regarded as sources of inspiration.
In the chapter entitled „Ruhe, jetzt wird gearbeitet", we see how
the author's close contact with nature fails to provide a tonic
for his hypersensitiveness and nervousness which, for the duration
of his creative activities, demand the strict imposition of a ban on
all noises produced by man or animal in the house and on the
farm – („Olsch", as we have seen, breaks the ban with impunity).
Such, in many instances, is the author's mental and physical state
after the completion of a novel, that he is forced to spend a few
weeks recuperating in a hospital: „Denn ich hasse es, hinter
einem Roman als kranker, von völliger Schlaflosigkeit geplagter
Mann in einem Sanatorium herumzuliegen. Ich habe Angst vor
jenem Zustand der Überreizung, in dem mich schon die Fliege
an der Wand ärgert." [6] Furthermore, the author experiences no
relief from the rather oppressive and self-imposed compulsion of
having to fulfil a certain quota of written pages each day. When
those six pages of his *Tagespensum* have been filled, he lays down
his pen and no stimulus seems present or strong enough to impel
him to continue, except, perhaps, the incentive provided by the
apparently exulting thought of producing a few more pages which
will be credited to his *Pensum* of the following day. This sounds
like a mechanical process indeed. The success of Fallada's creative
process does, in fact, seem to depend to a greater degree on such
outward matters as the choice of the right kind of tobacco for his
pipe and the condition of his fountain pen than on the state of his
mental outlook or on any restorative or stimulating forces absor-
bed from his contact with nature. Not a word, in fact, is said
about these forces. The omission is not only revealing from a
political point of view, but it is also in perfect accord with our
author's blended attitude towards life. Such an attitude prevented
Fallada from extolling the supposedly magic resources of a life
he was too famililiar with to be able to sentimentalise.

What function, then, does Hans Fallada's cherished rustic

6 *Ibid.*, p. 195.

talisman perform for him? It would seem that his return to the country constituted first and foremost a retreat into complete solitude and an escape from a world filled with problems he was no longer able to cope with. Musing on his imminent departure from his little estate, he writes in *Heute bei uns zu Haus:* „Mahlendorf ade – gutes altes Dorf an fünf Seen, umrauscht von Wäldern, Trösteinsamkeit, ade!" [7] It was this „Trösteinsamkeit" which Hans Fallada primarily sought and indeed found by moving into the country and onto a small peasant holding which was, characteristically, completely isolated from the rest of the sur-rounding inhabitants. From this point of view, life in the country undoubtedly served a useful purpose for the author and furnished him with a congenial milieu. It was within the framework of the simple pattern of country life, isolated from the complexities and tensions of crowded urban living, that Fallada could hope to retain some measure of inner stability and to gather the strength he required to overcome his many spiritual struggles.

Martha Dodd, who in her book *Through Embassy Eyes* (1939) calls Hans Fallada „the one remaining author of recognized talent writting in Germany", relates her impression of a visit to our authors' little farm in Mecklenburg in the following manner:

We finally found the village and managed to struggle through the bad roads until we arrived at the modest cottage set by the lake and surrounded by a few acres of cultivated land.

Hans Fallada came out with his buxom, simple wife to meet us ... He was a stockily built man with blondish hair and charming, genial features; ... Their life seemed to be built around their family and their farm. He was isolated from life and happy in his isolation. There was some discussion and though I got the impression that he was not and could not be a Nazi – what artist is? – I felt a certain resignation in his attitude.

. . . .

This withdrawal from life was Hans Fallada's tragic solution to the problems that might have been troubling his peace. It was a temp-tation to which he had completely succumbed. And the impression of defeatism he gave us was saddening. [8]

---

[7] *Ibid.,* p. 266.
[8] Martha Dodd, *Through Embassy Eyes* (New York, Harcourt, Brace and Company, 1939), pp. 84–85.

Saddening indeed this impression must have been. But at a time when all free expessions of independent opinions were being brutally suppressed and when he himself was being drawn into the midst of the controversies of a political system so alien to his own way of thinking, Hans Fallada saw no other alternative but to accept a solution which was most congenial to him and which Martha Dodd, with some justification, chooses to call a tragic one. It was a solution which provided Fallada with at least the remnants of a sense of security and belonging and indeed with the confidence that certain incorruptible and eternal values still existed in a world that seemed to be completely out of joint. Such simple experiences as the gathering of mushrooms in the silent and mysterious woods or the observing of a swarm of his beloved bees were capable of generating a genuine feeling of deep joy in him tantamount almost to the bliss that springs from those rare and blessed moments of the dawning of some divine revelation:

Welch seltsames Glück! Was ist es denn, das einem das Herz schneller klopfen macht, wenn man das Gesicht über die von fremdem Leben wimmelnde Wabe neigt, dieses Gesicht, von dem die Tiere nichts wissen – ?
. . . .
Viel weiter her, aus viel tieferen Gründen des Seins muß dieses Glück kommen. Neigt vielleicht zu dieser Stunde Gott sein Antlitz über die Wabe Welt, sieht wimmelndes Leben, und lächelt – von ferne? Ach es ist ein seltsam seliges Glück ein bißchen Herrgott zu sein ⊥ über einer Bienenwabe! [9]

It was experiences such as these, with their quality of timelessness and universality, that provided, if not the sovereign remedy, at least an effective lenitive for the author's troubled mind.

  We shall turn now to consider Hans Fallada's presentation of the theme of the return to the soil in some of his other novels and try to determine to what extent the rustic way of living as opposed to city living is regarded as the source of healthy and conserving forces and as the remedy for some of the pressing problems of modern man's social life. In *Bauern, Bonzen und*

---

[9] *Heute bei uns zu Haus,* p. 129.

Bomben the country is brought into direct conflict with the city. The novel, as the author tells us in its preface, deals with the war of each against all. As the narrative progresses, however, it becomes apparent that it is more specifically a war of the „boden-ständige Volk" against the injustices of the „Verwaltungsapparat" and the two-faced political intrigues of the state, represented by its scheming and dishonest officials in the city. The gulf which separates the rural inhabitants from the city-dwellers proves to be of such dimensions that no amount of understanding and no number of attempts at conciliation and compromise succeed in bridging it. The intense friction between the peasants on the one hand and the *Bonzen* on the other result in nothing short of a resort to violence of which the peasants are seen as the innocent victims. Hans Fallada's sympathies in this book are quite obviously with the cause of the peasants who are portrayed as basically law-abiding, obedient and maltreated citizens. As one of the peasants puts it: „Das charakterisiert die heutige Regierung. Die Ultraroten und die Nazis dürfen alles, wir Bauern stehen unter Ausnahmerecht." [10] This, incidentally, is not the only passage in the book criticising the political bumbling of the Weimar Repu-blic. Not only the first part of the last sentence of the above quotation but the statement in its entirety was, as could be expec-ted, struck from the 1938 edition of the novel, which contains a rather apologetic introduction by the author.

In *Bauern, Bonzen und Bomben* Fallada points out that the peasants have no acclaimed leader, yet, in contrast to the disunity of the political factions in the city, they display a strong sense of solidarity and a union of common aspirations. He stresses also their familiarity and close contact with traditions and ancient rites which have been wrecked and have become extinct in city societies, and he constantly points to the strong spiritual bond between the peasant and his surroundings, between man and nature. This becomes particularly apparent when Fallada relates the meeting of a *Thing* to which the peasants have been sum-moned in order to conclude a boycott against the city. The great

[10]   *Bauern, Bonzen und Bomben*, p. 156.

assembly of peasants gathers by the light of the moon in eerie and almost primeval surroundings:

Padberg hat den Ort gefunden für den Thing. Hinaus aus den Tanzsälen der Wirtschaften mit den verblaßten Papiergirlanden, dem Geruch von Bier und Tabak, dem grünen Bretterwerk der Emporen, den Erinnerungen an Weiber und Musike!
Dort, wo die spärlichen hohen Schirmkiefern stehen, der Ginster gelb wuchert, zwischen den dunklen Massen des Wacholders die verstreuten Blöcke eines auseinandergeworfenen Hünengrabes liegen – dort, wenn es Nacht wird (und der Mond steht im Kalender), und es ist etwas Wind und fünftausend Bauern und ein Gerichtsthing.[11]

The contrast between the artificiality of the city milieu and the unadulterated environment in which the countryfolk are perfectly in harmony with the mysteries and timeless rhythms of nature is clearly made. And Hans Fallada holds a shielding hand over a fuller and more basic life, charged with more genuine experiences than those encountered within the stone-bound limits of an urban society. On one occassion in the novel he makes perfectly sure that the uplifted boot of a city-official, trudging down a country-road on an errand to confiscate the cattle of a tax-evading peasant, is withdrawn and prevented from crushing the symbol of life and timeless beauty resting in the dust below in the form of a butterfly:

„Halt! Einen Augenblick!" ruft Thiel und hält den Kollegen am Arm. Im Staub sitzt ein Schmetterling, ein braunbuntes Pfauenauge mit zitternden Flügeln. Seine Fühler bewegen sich tastend in der Sonne, im Licht, in der Wärme.
Und Kalübbe zieht den Fuß zurück, der schon über dem Tier schwebte. Zieht ihn zurück und bleibt stehen, sieht hinab auf den beseelten farbigen Staub.
„Ja, auch das gibt es, Thiel", sagt er erleichtert. „Weiß Gott, Sie haben recht. Auch das gibt es. Und manchmal wird der Fuß zurückgezogen." [12]

The author's own close acquaintance with all the problems of both rustic and urban life prevented him, however, from present-

---

[11] *Ibid.*, pp. 224–225.
[12] *Ibid.*, pp. 23–24.

ing a mere black and white contrast. Fallada is far from regarding the peasant and his way of living as the perfect model of a healthy and uncorrupted existence. There are incidents of unmitigated brutality which occur in the country such as, for instance, the vicious reprisals of the villagers against a peasant who has dared to act countrary to their common cause by buying a clock in the city and thus breaking the boycott. Again, the only murder which occurs in the book is committed by a hot-headed and brutal peasant, a perfect tyrant of his family and household.

Hans Fallada's sane and blended approach to the problems encountered in the country as well as in the city is apparent throughout his entire work. In *Wir hatten mal ein Kind,* a novel patterned on the central theme of the reconquest of the ancestral farm, Fallada, as noted in the preceding chapter, creates a memorable portrait of a ruthless young farmer, Hannes Gäntschow. We are told that young Gäntschow's ancestors had always been the terror of the neighbourhood, living in complete isolation and self-sufficiency and protected from their neighbours by a pack of vicious dogs. We are hardly given the impression of people leading a healthier and more rewarding life in the country than in the city when we hear that: „die Gäntschows seien noch heute die reinen Heiden, mit Saufen, Strandgutstehlen, Wildern und Huren. Und Malte Gäntschow, der Großvater, hat noch entschuldigend von sich gegrient: Wir sind ja man gestern erst Christen geworden, Herre." [13] Young Johannes Gäntschow proves to be no better than his forefathers. When he returns to the island with his young wife, Elise, he immediately sets out on the task of restoring the decayed farm. He has to acquit himself of the same task a few years later when his estranged wife uses the years of his absence, spent in utter solitude in the company of his old love, Christiane, to bring complete destruction to the estate. But Gäntschow, who has developed into a cold-blooded egotist, acquits himself excellently of the task on both occassions, and the methods he uses to achieve his aims are simply ruthlessness and brutality. The only redeeming feature of Gäntschow's cha-

[13] *Wir hatten mal ein Kind,* p. 12.

racter is his profound love for the land, for the „Äcker". One might be tempted to assume that Hans Fallada is in this book in fact paying homage, in the manner of the „blood and soil" ideology, to the conception of the natural hero, who may walk over corpses as long as he attains his goals. This, however, is most certainly not the case. For, as we have already pointed out, the author shows how the egotism and brutality of Hannes Gäntschow alienates him from everyone, even from the two women who love him, and leaves him in complete isolation with but the bitter memory of a loveless life plaguing his conscience: „Sein ganzes Leben lag vor ihm, klar, kalt, eine Schnee- und eine Eiswüste. Keine Blume." [14] In the case of Gäntschow a rustic environment certainly fails to produce the kind of experiences that are the essential ingredients of a full and truly rewarding existence. Clearly Fallada intimates in this novel that there are other important forces, spiritual and intellectual forces above all else, that are required to give birth to and to sustain such a meaningful life.

In *Wolf unter Wölfen* Hans Fallada's rustic talisman again becomes ineffective or is, at least, not relied upon exclusively. This voluminous novel, which aimed at being the narrative on an epic scale of the great German Inflation period, brings both the country and the city on to its immense canvas. The first volume bears the title „Die Stadt und ihre Ruhelosen" while the second book is entitled „Das Land in Brand", thus indicating that it was not only the urban population which was victimised by all the disastrous consequences of this abnormal epoch of German social history. Life in the country provides no adequate safeguard against these disrupting aftergrowths. We are shown clearly how inflation destroyed also the morals of the agrarian population and the times were just as terribly out of joint on the land as in the cities.

The scene in this very intricate narrative alternates between Berlin and an estate in East Prussia. In the opening chapters, Wolfgang Pagel's and Petra's environment is that of the city

14 *Ibid.*, p. 539.

society of Berlin, which is vividly pictured as a maze of depravity, made up of corruption, vice, prostitution, gambling, hunger and general demoralisation. Fallada's narrative vigour is at its very peak in these sections of the book. Then there is a shift to the country, where young Pagel is employed on an estate. On the surface and upon initial contact with the soil and nature the peace of the countryside does in fact seem to furnish restorative forces for the disillusioned creatures of a corrupt urban society. In an exuberant mood the ex-officer, von Studmann, conjurs up a vision of salvation as he exclaims to Pagel:

Wissen Sie es nicht? Der Friede der Felder, der Atem der Natur, gewachsener Boden unter den Füßen – Sie wissen es nicht, was es heißt, täglich dreißig Kilometer mit brennenden Sohlen die stupiden Gänge eines Hotels entlang zu preschen ...
Berlin! Verruchtes, vergessenes Berlin!

It is significant, however, that he himself immediately destroys this idyllic vision when he continues:

Ich ahne ja schon, auch dieser Friede ist nur Schwindel. In den so malerisch ins Grüne geduckten Häusern des lieblichen Dörfleins dort werden Klatschsucht, Neid, Angeberei zu Hause sein, wie in jeder großstädtischen Mietskaserne! ... – Aber, Mitmensch Pagel, lassen Sie mir mein Glück, entblättern Sie nicht die junge Blüte meines Glaubens! Friede der Felder, Eintracht der Hütten, Ruhe der Natur. [15]

And indeed, the ostensible peace of the fields turns out to be but a pleasant delusion and the vision of salvation an empty bubble. For in the country, too, the general disillusionment and corruption of the time make themselves felt. Here, too, disorder and hatred amongst the people predominate; here, too, illegal activities, such as the military undertakings of the „Schwarze Reichswehr" led by young ex-officers, thrive and contribute to the general disruption of the peace. The rural communities prove as susceptible to all the corrupting influences of the day as any urban society: „Unzufriedenheit, Haß, Verzweiflung gibt es genug

---

[15] *Wolf unter Wölfen*, II, 548–549.

auf dem Lande. Die Banknotenpresse in Berlin schleudert mit jeder neuen Woge Papiergeld eine neue Woge Erbitterung ins Land." [16] The city, then, is clearly seen as the main source and centre of the disquiet, but the country fails as well to ward off the spreading infection. The quest for survival proves to be the paramount concern of all the parties involved in the bitter battle of all against all.

The picture which Hans Fallada paints in this novel is that of the total moral collapse of all sections of the German population under the Weimar Republic. At such times of crisis, the author refuses to turn in an idealistic fashion to the resources of a more or less imaginary natural life as to a magic fountain, gushing forth with rejuvenating and healing waters. Fallada realises quite clearly that his highly-regarded rural talisman may often turn out to be but an ineffective and fantastic device. Significantly, in *Wolf unter Wölfen*, it is a city relationship, young Pagel's love for the girl from the streets, Petra, that ultimately saves him from total disillusionment and leads him on towards rehabilitation and a new life. This is not to say, however, that the rural environment and the search for harmony with nature do not play very important roles in moulding Pagel's character. It is, after all, only after he has been fully exposed to these influences that he matures into a well-balanced and forward-looking individual, fully conscious of his rightful position in society and his responsibilities towards his fellow beings.

The fairy tale *Märchen vom Stadtschreiber, der aufs Land flog* again introduces the theme of the restoration of an ancestral farm which has fallen into the hands of unrightful owners and, connected with this theme, the motif of the return to nature. The clerk, Guntram Spatt, is induced by his colleague, Bubo, to change into a sparrow (the „little man" of the bird world, one might say) and to fly from his dull and stifling work to the „Spatzenhof" of which he is the rightful heir. The transformation, as mentioned earlier, takes place by means of a magic brown „Haupthaar" plucked from a sparrow. This sparrow, in turn, is transformed into a

---

[16] *Ibid.*, I, 391.

human being and takes Guntrams's place at his desk in the form
of an identical and, as it turns out later, wicked alter ego. Freeing
himself from the fetters of his mechanical existence and flying
into the country as a „free" sparrow does not, however, bring the
desired deliverance for the alienated „little man". Having arrived
at the farm, where he reconverts himself into a human being,
Guntram soon realises that the country, too, is infested with
hatred and inhabited by two-faced and intriguing people. It is
these intrigues which finally succeed in ejecting Guntram and
his uncle and cousin from their property. Here, too, then, there
proves to be no security from the falsehoods and disruptions of
the time, and the flight to the country certainly does not solve
all the problems bedevilling the wearied city-dweller, Guntram
Spatt.

Certain elements in this clever allegory indicate that it is
clearly, besides being a satire on the forces of National Socialism,
also intended as a mild parody of the dilemma which so often
faces nature-hungry modern man, who, when placed in a rustic
milieu, either through insensitivity or simply because he has
become too „civilised", finds himself, to his own astonishment and
dismay, sorrily out of tune with that kind of an environment. This
is, for instance, brought out in the contrast between the delicate
Schreiberlein and the rough farm-hand, Enak, who is blessed
with a more than robust physique but a not so healthy mind.
Enak, highly sceptical as he is from the start of Guntram's abilities
to run a farm, tests his competence by making him draw water
from the well at a murderous pace. Guntram, of course, fails
miserably to stand the test and is comforted by his uncle with
the following words: „Nun zürne ihm nicht, daß er Dich ein
wenig pusten gemacht, der einfache Landmann will dem Stadt-
herrn nicht wohl, von dem er glaubt, seine weichen Händchen
verrichteten nichts Rechtes, wie ja auch der Städter den Landmann oft verächtlich einen Mistknollen schimpft." [17] At the end
of the story, after Guntram has been changed into a human being
again, Fallada speaks tenderly of the „gute Mutter Erde" having

[17]   *Märchen vom Stadtschreiber, der aufs Land flog*, p. 47.

played an important part in the development that finds its climax in what amounts to the birth of a new man.

In *Kleiner Mann – großer Mann, alles vertauscht* the „little man's" move to the country, where he has inherited an estate, does not prove salutary for the parties concerned. Again the country turns out to be as susceptible to corruption and depravity as any urban environment could possibly be; and it is only after he has given up his wealth and returned to his old occupation in the city that the „little man", Max Schreyvogel, regains his security and moral responsibility.

In some of Fallada's novels, however, his attitude towards the „return to nature" call is not as sceptical and guarded as in the works we have just discussed. Quite often this call is shown to live up to its promises of rejuvenation and spiritual rebirth which it holds in store for those who will but follow it. In *Kleiner Mann – was nun?* Hans Fallada offers effective solace to his jobless „little man" by moving him out of the insecurity of the city and settling his family on a garden plot in the outskirts, and he shows how Pinneberg draws strength from such simple yet reassuring experiences as watching the rushing, clear waters of a hurrying brook with his son: „Den Murkel an der Hand, trat Pinneberg an das Bachbett und sie sahen beide lange stumm auf das strömende eilige Wasser. Nach einiger Zeit sagte Pinneberg: „Das ist das Wasser, mein Murkel, das gute liebe Wasser." [18] For Pinneberg the flowing water becomes a symbol of the constancy and immutability of certain eternal laws of nature the knowledge of which engenders a feeling of confidence and hopefulness. In the end, Pinneberg's little shack and its surrounding garden become a last stable refuge and stronghold for the family, harbouring hope and providing a firm basis for a renewed attempt to cope with the puzzling problems of the day.

In *Altes Herz geht auf die Reise* (1936) the reinvigorating forces which old Professor Kittguss absorbs from his contact with nature are clearly perceivable. The novel is again patterned on the theme of the reconquest of a farm from its unrightful posses-

[18] *Kleiner Mann – was nun?*, p. 325.

sors. A message written by his young godchild, Rosemarie, and
imploring his help, induces the old intellectual to abandon his
dusty manuscripts and obscure biblical studies and to step out
into the freshening breeze of the open countryside. And it is here,
in the company of the village children. who have banded together
in support of Rosemarie's fight against her wicked foster parents,
that old Kittguss undergoes a profound process of spiritual
rejuvenation. His experience of nature and of the bond that
unites all living creation becomes tantamount to a deep religious
revelation. The dawning of this insight occurs as he stands cn a
fence in the midst of a forest, gazing out across the land:

Und von seinem erhöhten Standort sah der Professor weit in das
Land, über Wälder und Felder . . .
Ihm war es plötzlich, als stehe er auf der Kanzel, und wenn ihm
damals in seinen milchjungen Tagen der Predigttext manche Schwie-
rigkeit gemacht hatte, hier fiel ihm gleich der sanfte Heilige Franzis-
kus ein – und er, der sein Leben in einer grauen Steinstadthöhle ver-
bracht hatte, hörte nun mit rechten Ohren den freundlichen Lobgesang von meiner lieben Schwester, der Quelle, und vom Bruder
Wind: von der Gemeinschaft alles Lebenden. Und er hätte in diesen
Lobgesang mit einstimmen können, ohne textliche Vorbereitung, doch
aus vollem Herzen . . .
. . . .
Eben war es noch die Vikariatskanzel gewesen, und nun war der
Zauntritt schon das Lehrpult am Königlichen Prinz-Joachim Gymna-
sium zu Berlin-Schöneberg an der Grunewaldstraße. All die jungen
Knabengesichter sahen erwartungsvoll zu ihm auf, und er versuchte,
sie sanft und behutsam in den Geist der Schrift einzuführen, in ein
werktätiges Christentum. Wie war er von diesem Wege doch so weit
abgekommen?! Unter dem sachte schaukelnden Herbsthimmel wurde
„das gemütliche, stille Gelehrtenzimmer" in der Akazienstraße zu dem,
was es war, zu einer grauen, dunklen Höhle der Eigensucht und der
Unfruchtbarkeit. [19]

Here, then, the immediate experience of nature helps to clear
away the obstructions which hypothetical speculations place in
the path that leads to a truer understanding of man's existence
and of his relationship to his creator. Old Kittguss experiences

---

[19] *Altes Herz geht auf die Reise* (Berlin, Rowohlt Verlag, 1936), pp.
166–167.

a process of spiritual and intellectual clarification. Nature becomes the great educator, freeing man from the fetters of doubt and scepticism and engendering „ein erhöhtes Lebens – und Kraftgefühl".

On various occasions in this novel, which gives ample evidence of Fallada's indebtedness to German Romanticism, our author does, however, come precariously close to succumbing to a somewhat sentimental vision of a natural state of human perfection and purity which may be attained on earth, particularly when conditions are such that closeness to nature constitutes a significant feature of one's daily life. This utopian conception becomes all too opparent in his portrayal of the village children, and especially that of Rosemarie. The nostalgic *Heimweh* for the lost innocence of our childhood, coupled with the assumption that the child has the potential of a saintlike existence and is good simply by virtue of its childhood, is all too obvious in the juxtaposition of the weary old scholar and his young godchild. For Professor Kittguss, Rosemarie assumes all the qualities of a saintly, almost supernatural being:

Sie stand da, und seltsam war sie anzuschauen in ihrer verschmuddelten, mißfarbigen Magdtracht mit den Holzpantoffeln an den Füßen. Aber auf den schmalen Schultern saß ein schöner, zierlicher Kopf mit einem sehr kleinen, blaßroten Mund . . .

Aber das alles war es nicht. Es waren auch nicht die zartfarbenen, sanft gerundeten Wangen, sondern es war der ferne, wie wesenlose, wie unirdische Blick der Augen, die blaugrau waren, ein Blick, der durch die Dinge hindurch zu gehen schien, bis weit, weit hinter diese.

Dieser Blick war es, der den alten Mann ergriffen hatte; . . .

Vor diesem Blick war das Böse, das ihm von ihr erzählt worden war, lügenhaft geworden, denn die Kinder des andern Reichs, das nicht auf dieser Erde ist, erkennen einander wohl. [20]

It is these simple country-children, who harbour „kein Falsch" in their hearts, coupled with the invigorating experience of a close contact with nature, that work the miracle of the old professor's rejuvenation and mental rebirth.

[20]   *Ibid.,* p. 36.

Even in this book, however, Fallada remains well aware of the different picture which comes to view when one glances at the other side of the coin. For the country-folk also count among their members such brutal and ignorant characters as Rosemarie's foster parents, the Schliekers, who torture their children and light their fires with pages torn from priceless books. If Fallada points clearly to the damage which life in a „Steinstadthöhle", divorced from the tangible realities of everyday existence, may do to man's spiritual life and sense of awareness and displays a distinct anti-*Bildung* sentiment by implicitly criticising an educational system of which Kittguss is a representative *par excellence,* it is equally true that he also shows the deplorable consequences of a lack of all elements of cultural life. In the end it is, after all, the ineradicable goodness and love of the old intellectual which proves to be instrumental in the restoration of peace and justice. *Altes Herz geht auf die Reise* contains some of Hans Fallada's most profound thoughts on the whole question of man's tendency to seek reassurance in an area of genuine and uncorrupted relations, away from the distortions of modern society. This is, in fact, the only novel in which Fallada attaches religious meaning to this problem of modern man's flight from a mechanical existence.

Nature again performs an educating and healing function in *Jeder stirbt für sich allein* as Fallada, in the midst of an account of terror-ruled Nazi Germany, inserts a *Zwischenspiel* entitled „Ein Idyll auf dem Lande". It is to the country that Eva Kluge takes her refuge from the instability and terror of Berlin. This simple woman, whose daily duty had been that of delivering mail which brought sorrow and distress to almost every door she knocked at, regains her „innere Ruhe" in the country. And it is here, too, that she later adopts the wayward boy, Kuno-Dieter, who has escaped from the great city and his parents and has taken to leading the life of a tramp. The restorative forces to which young Kuno-Dieter becomes exposed in the country help to provide him with a new sense of direction and equip him with the mental stability he requires to build a new and brighter future for himself: „Er hat viel gelernt hier auf dem Lande, und er hat auch – gottlob –fast ebensoviel vergessen." [21]

Ein Mann will hinauf is the story of a young and very ambitious man from the country who sets out to „conquer Berlin". Karl Siebrecht proves perfectly capable of standing his own ground in the vicious and competitive fight for success in a great city. Here we have the theme of *Stadtflucht* reversed. Even though Siebrecht never regrets his *Landflucht* and does not return to the country as a repentant son to the comforting maternal embrace, he does experience a deep sense of loss on the occasion of a short visit to the happy grounds of his childhood days. Confronted with the breathing, pregnant earth, the richness of the ripening fields and the animals grazing in the meadows, he suddenly realises that life in the city and his struggle for prestige and success have alienated him from all true values and from experiences which constitute the very essence of life itself:

Plötzlich fiel ihm ein, wie lange er keine reifen Getreidefelder gesehen hatte und keine weidenden Kühe. Als er in Berlin war, hatte er nicht daran gedacht, es hatte ihm nicht gefehlt, aber nun, da er es wiedersah, merkte er, es hatte ihm eben doch gefehlt. Nur Steine hatte er gehabt, Steine und Menschen. Nein, keine Menschen ... nur Leute. Ein Gewimmel von Leuten. Und er hatte mitgewimmelt ...

Alte verkrüppelte Weiden standen am Weg, und rechts und links breiteten sich reifende Felder aus, die Kartoffeln blühten schon, und dazwischen ging dieses Kind – jeder Schritt hinterließ eine Spur in dem weichen Sande. Er war über die harten Granitplatten gelaufen, die keine Spur annahmen, nichts zeugte von ihm ... Diese Felder waren ewig, immer wieder würden die Weiden ausschlagen. Immer wieder würden kleine Kinderfüße sich im Sand abzeichnen – ewig! [22]

It is the same conclusion reached by Gäntschow in *Wir hatten mal ein Kind,* when he speaks of the land being „unzerstörbar". Here, then, the impersonal and transitory nature of city life and of the casual human relationships established in an urban society is clearly contrasted to a life involving elemental experiences and obligations and entailing daily contact with incorruptible natural

[21] *Jeder stirbt für sich allein,* p. 536.
[22] *Ein Mann will hinauf,* pp. 317–318.

phenomena which become symbols of eternal values and engender a reassuring sense of security and permanence. It is, ultimately, the constant attempt to awaken an awareness of these timeless aspects of man's existence that underlies Hans Fallada's preoccupation with and interpretation of the theme of modern man's urge to seek a fuller life by returning to the soil.

Although Hans Fallada always displays an extremely sceptical attitude towards the values and pretenses by which all sections of human society function, he refrains from preaching any philosophy which claims to hold man's salvation in store. In some instances, as we have seen, Fallada's rustic talisman performs a useful function and provides the conserving and regenerative forces for which modern man is searching; but quite often it simply fails and proves ineffective. It is clear, then, that our author certainly did not see salvation for mankind in general and Germany in particular in a return to an agrarian state with the peasant as its backbone. Nor could he possibly ally himself to the accompanying „biological" view of human nature, which contends that man is healthy as long as he continues to lead a „natural" life, that is to say, to live like a beast of prey. Hans Fallada was in his general outlook too liberal-minded to be able to take a liking to such reactionary views. We might add that he was also too much of a „realist" in terms of his *Weltanschauung* and his conditioning through personal experiences to permit us to identify his aims with those of the majority of *Heimatdichter*, whose basic disposition is, after all, to a large extent escapist and „sentimentalisch" in the Schillerian sense.

If we should require additional proof that Hans Fallada, even though he did to a certain extent follow the „back to nature" cry, was certainly not in tune with the „blood and soil" ideology, the excellent satirical portrait of a „Blut und Boden" writer in *Wer einmal aus dem Blechnapf frißt* will furnish it. The scene deserves to be quoted at this point. It is that in which Willi Kufalt confronts the *Heimatschriftsteller*, Malte Scialoja, whose exotic name is telling in itself. Scialoja has held out a promise of help to the unemployed ex-convict, but he fails miserably to live up to his pledge and displays a singular lack of sympathy for and understanding of the real problems of the „einfache Volk" of whom he claims to be the representative:

Scialoja ist ein blasser Mann mit einem untadligen dunklen Scheitel, in einem Lüsterjackett. Er hört auf die Tanzmelodien, er liest auch mal ein paar Zeilen aus den Manuskripten, und dann sieht er sich seine Nägel an. Er ist ein großer Mann, er weiß das sehr genau. Es ist nicht einfach, das Leben eines großen Mannes zu führen. Man hat seine Verpflichtungen. Das hat er immer verstanden.

. . . .

Er horcht auf die Radiomusik. Die spielen Tänze. Es sind jene bösen falschen Tänze, die dem Volk so schaden. Es gibt so hübsche Bauerntänze, all das ist verdrängt von diesem Asphaltkitsch. Aber er horcht darauf. Es hört sich nicht schlecht an, aber es ist schlecht. Schon klopft es wieder an die Tür.

. . . .

„Also – Sie wollen?" fragt Scialoja und schreibt weiter. „Ich habe Ihnen das ausführlich in meinem ersten Brief auseinandergesetzt", antwortet Kufalt zögernd.

. . . .

Und er setzt leiser hinzu: „Ich habe Ihnen doch geschrieben, ich bin vorbestraft. Ich finde nichts. Ich dachte, daß gerade Sie..."

. . . .

„Dutzende von Vorbestraften kommen zu mir um Hilfe, ich sage Ihnen, Dutzende"....
Kufalt steht abwartend...
„Sehen Sie", sagt der große Mann, „ich habe zu arbeiten, ich vertrete das Volk, das einfache Volk, verstehen Sie. Blut und Scholle, verstehen Sie?"
„Ja", antwortet Kufalt geduldig.
„Ich darf mich nicht zersplittern", sagt der andere weiter.
„Ich habe einen Beruf. Verstehen Sie, was Berufung heißt?"
„Ja", sagt Kufalt wieder. [23]

How far removed Scialoja's view of himself as a representative of the simple folk and of the „Scholle" is from Hans Fallada's basic beliefs and concerns is too obvious to require any elaboration.

Hans Fallada's criticism of modern social and cultural values, whether they be represented by an urban or by a rural society, is characterised by a *Sachlichkeit* which nevertheless makes us

[23] *Wer einmal aus dem Blechnapf frißt*, pp. 297–299.

constantly aware of the author's personal likes and aversions and which all too frequently betrays a strong emotional undercurrent. The elementary life close to nature obviously exerted a very strong attraction upon our author, and he himself returned to the soil and retreated to the simple pattern of life on his farm. An element of escapism is doubtless present in this withdrawal to what he called his „Trösteinsamkeit". We might be inclined to feel that it is even less fortunate to see Fallada escape also in some of his writings into a realm of what is often rather whimsical and insubstantial speculation. It is true that books such as the modern fairy tales *Hoppelpoppel – wo bist du?* (1936) and *Geschichten aus der Murkelei* (1938) as well as many of the stories collected in the *Gesammelte Erzählungen* and even to a certain extent a novel like *Kleiner Mann –großer Mann, alles vertauscht* are the products of such speculation, which many would consider to be so alien to a „realistic" writer like Fallada. But Hans Fallada's varied and often contradictory work is perhaps the best illustration of the very dilemma that characterises man in our century, torn as he is between having to cope „realistically" and plausibly with the realities of a highly impersonal and mechanised world and his inevitable yearning to seek salvation by escaping to a less complex yet more genuine and rewarding existence.

IV

THE ISOLATION OF THE INDIVIDUAL

Throughout Hans Fallada's entire work there are recurrent indications of his absorption in the problem of the isolation of the individual in society. The feeling of solitude, of social and spiritual loneliness, dominates almost all of his main characters, and the little word „allein" is one which finds no equal in the frequency of its occurrence in our author's work.

Our main concern in this chapter will be to discuss Fallada's interpretation of the problem of the isolation of the individual, to see what different forms this isolation takes in his works and to inquire what views he either implicitly or explicitly expressed on this problem. Did Hans Fallada regard such notions as isolationism, individualism, the freedom of the individual soul, individual self-assertion and self-sufficiency as ideals worthy of being upheld at all costs, or did he, rather, consider them to be more of a curse than a blessing to the individual? What are the forces which Hans Fallada suggests as the means of overcoming the isolation of the individual? What is his concept of society, his ideal of human social intercourse? And what, if anything, has Fallada to say about the isolation of the individual in that realm where he transcends the limited social sphere of a human community? What has he to say, that is, about the spiritual isolation of the individual, the loneliness and freedom of the individual soul in the region of the mind and the spirit? What, further, has he to say about the individual's ultimate religious transcendence and its social relevance? These are the basic questions that will concern us in our subsequent investigation.

We have already noted that Hans Fallada was himself a badly

balanced, extreme individualist. In his autobiographical novel *'Heute bei uns zu Haus* he goes so far as to bluntly refer to himself as „der erwige alte Egoist". Further evidence from this novel shows clearly that Fallada felt his individualism to be more of a burden than a blessing and that he longed for some means to overcome his self-chosen isolation. He was forever on the retreat into a place and life of his own; he was Robinson living on an island without a Friday, and even though in the chapter entitled „Robinson", in *Der Alpdruck,* he assures us that this Robinson dreaded nothing more than the prospect of being rescued from his island of solitude, Fallada's other autobiographical accounts give convincing evidence of the fact that he also yearned for nothing more than for someone to deliver him from his bitter aloneness and to point him the way into human community. Thus in the portrait of his eldest son in *Heute bei uns zu Haus* he writes:

Ich entdecke an ihm wie an mir den gleichen Hang, sich zu isolieren, die gleiche Leidenschaft, Menschen zu beobachten.

. . . .

– dieser Junge hat einen schweren Weg vor sich, das weiß ich, sein Vater.

. . . .

Ich sah den einsamen Weg vor ihm, den ich gegangen war, den er würde gehen müssen, wenn er solch Einzelgänger blieb.

. . . .

Und ich erinnerte mich, wie in den zwanziger Jahren mich die selbstgewählte Einsamkeit wie ein glühender Schmerz plagte, wie ich Abend für Abend von einem Caféhaus ins andere lief, oft an einem Abend in zwölf, fünfzehn Stück . . . Da saß ich dann und sah angstvoll in jedes Gesicht, ob es nicht endlich das Gesicht des Menschen sein würde, der mich erlöste. Jedem Eintretenden sah ich entgegen, und hinter jedem Fortgehenden hätte ich hinterdrein laufen mögen, ihn auf der Straße um ein wenig Wärme und Gemeinschaft anzusprechen.

. . . .

Wahrhaftig, ich kannte die tiefe Wunde, die ein Einzelgängerschicksal dem Betroffenen selbst und allen ihn Anhängenden bereitet! Ich weiß, daß diese Wunde nie ganz verheilt. Und ich war entschlossen, meinen Sohn nicht diesen Weg gehen zu lassen. [1]

---

[1] *Heute bei uns zu Haus,* pp. 252–254.

Hans Fallada, then, had experienced „die tiefe Wunde, die ein Einzelgängerschicksal dem Betroffenen selbst und allen ihm Anhängenden bereitet", and there can be no doubt that he was constantly and indeed often morbidly searching for the human hand that would reach out and draw him from his isolation and was at all times acutely aware of the need for a communal spirit. Fallada's whole work, after all, furnishes the clearest and most conclusive evidence of the extent to which he had developed a „social conscience". In all his novels Fallada never fails to sound a note of true compassion and to exhibit his profound sympathy with the whole common and, in many cases, degraded clay of humanity. Surely, no one can fail to perceive how firmly he believed that, in some measure, we must all be our brother's keeper if he is in need of sympathy and help. And yet Hans Fallada himself, throughout his sad life and to its tragic end, never really found a way out of his solitariness and into a communion with other human beings for whose struggles and hopes he had always displayed a deep *Mitleid*. Fallada remained forever isolated, socially and spiritually. This, indeed, is the supreme tragedy of his life.

We mentioned in our preceding chapter how Fallada withdrew to his little peasant holding in Mecklenburg, which was completely isolated from the rest of the surrounding inhabitants. Even though he cherished this retreat by the lake, he was also well aware of the strain this life of social isolation imposed on his family:

Saßen wir nicht hier allein in Mahlendorf, oft monatelang ohne jeden Verkehr, und hatte ich nicht Suse zu derselben Einsamkeit verurteilt, die mir nur durch meine Arbeit, durch den Umgang mit erdichteten Gestalten erträglich war, Suse, eine Frau, die sich nach Aussprache sehnte, die auch einmal in ein Theater oder Konzert wollte, zur gleichen monotonen Einsamkeit verdammt war! Hatte ich nicht jeden regelmäßigen nachbarlichen Verkehr, der sich doch etwa anbahnen wollte, immer wieder vereitelt? Sagte ich nicht heute noch beim angenehmsten Besuch: „Gerne sehe ich euch kommen, lieber sehe ich euch gehen – ?" [2]

[2] *Ibid.*, p. 253.

It was the „Umgang mit erdichteten Gestalten" which, for the greatest part of his life, constituted Hans Fallada's only companionship. Locked up in his study, his „Höhle" as he called it, he brought to life a world whose joys and sorrows he refused to share with any other person, not even with his beloved wife. In a creative process which Johannes R. Becher, in the article mentioned earlier, termed „ein unendlicher Schaffensprozess", and which the author himself in the essay „Wie ich Schriftsteller wurde" refers to as „ein Rausch über alle Räusche", Fallada brought forth his great novels out of the depth of an immensely creative imagination and in complete spiritual isolation. „Das ewige Reden" was never his favourite mode of expression and communication. And he would offer no one an opportunity to intrude into the sanctuary of his mind and consistently refused to speak about his inmost thoughts and his creative activity in general:

Was ich arbeite, womit ich umgehe, das weiß ich allein, bis die letzte Zeile des Buches geschrieben ist . . . .
Dies ist nichts, was ich mir etwa ausgedacht habe, ich kann einfach nicht darüber sprechen. Es ist mir verboten. Es ist ein Tabu. Allein muß ich sein, mit denen, die ich schaffe, allein will ich mit ihnen umgehen, die in mir entstehen, zum Leben erwachen.
   Nur in sehr geringem Maße ist mir die Gabe verliehen, mich durch Sprechen mitzuteilen. [3]

Hans Fallada, then, was an *Einzelgänger* on all levels of human endeavour. But he was an *Einzelgänger* who remained forever conscious of the need to overcome the loneliness of the individual by communal immersion. There can be no doubt that it was Fallada's innermost conviction that the individual must finally learn to live and toil for the sake of his fellow beings. The lone wolf among men must be tamed and brought to a sense of duty and obligation to the human community in which he lives. The following significant passage from *Heute bei uns zu Haus* makes Fallada's concept of society, his views on the position of the individual within the human family and his ideal of human

3 *Ibid.*, pp. 201–202.

social intercourse perfectly clear – though, of course, it might well be argued that one cannot altogether disregard the fact that these lines were written during the Hitler regime:

Damals, als ich aufwuchs, kurz nach der Jahrhundertwende, war der Einzelne alles. Man war sehr für Originale, das Individuum hatte ein Recht, sich auszuleben, ganz für sich allein etwas zu werden. Die ganze Gesellschaft bestand aus einer Schar Einzelmenschen. „So bin ich nun einmal – was soll ich dabei machen? Grade schön!" Heute ist der Einzelne nur das, was er im Dienst der Gesamtheit bedeutet und leistet. Die Eigenbrötler, die aus eigener Gnade und eigener Machtvollkommenheit nur dem eigenen Piepmatz Zucker geben, bedeuten nichts. In der Gemeinschaft soll der Mensch aufwachsen, für die Gemeinschaft wird er einst arbeiten, durch die Gemeinschaft ist er etwas. Sie gab ihm Sprache, Boden und Nahrung, er könnte isoliert von ihr nicht leben, nicht denken – also lebe er, denke er für sie!

Zu meinen Jugendzeiten hatte man eine (ganz falsche) Achtung vor Schrullen. Die Eltern sagten: „Er ist ein besonderes Kind!" Und die Lehrer meinten: „Er macht nicht recht mit, hat aber geistige Interessen!" Beide ließen das Kind, wie es war, sie hatten Respekt vor Eigenart (den man auch haben soll), aber sie hatten auch Respekt vor Schrullen, vor Menschenfeindlichkeit (den man ausrotten soll). [4]

It is particularly the last paragraph of the above quotation, with its important paranthetical comments, that deserves to be scrutinised; for it is here that our author states his views in all clarity. He notes categorically that the „Respekt vor Eigenart" should be upheld at all times. Hans Fallada had himself experienced the threat to the liberty of the individual's mind in the corporate state into which Germany had been formed by the National Socialists. He was only too aware of the disastrous consequences of the standardisation and regimentation of men's minds and, indeed, of all facets of human endeavour. Man's spiritual stature, then, must not be impinged upon. In the region of the mind the individual has a right and, indeed, a duty to maintain his freedom and absolute autonomy. Fallada clearly believed that the human mind needs this privacy and independence in order to be able to develop to its fullest capacity. He was aware, in other words,

[4] *Ibid.*, p. 254.

that the rebel minds, the unique creative instincts of each individual mind are absolutely essential for human and social development and should, therefore, be tolerated and protected. But when this „Respekt vor Eigenart" takes the form of „Respekt vor Schrullen, vor Menschenfeindlichkeit", then Fallada feels that some form of coercion is called for. Certainly our author would not give moral justification to that form of extreme individualism which develops into mere self-interest and self-affirmation for its own sake. Just how categorically Fallada rejected such anti-social individualism will become apparent when we turn our attention now to those of his novels in which he portrays an irreconcilable dissonance between the individual and the community and depicts the individual ruthlessly demanding and asserting his right to complete self-gratification. This group of novels comprises, as might be expected, most of the works which we discussed in our second chapter as depicting marital discord and the ultimate disintegration and failure of the marital relationship.

In *Wir hatten mal ein Kind* Hans Fallada shows the individual rigorously refusing to adapt himself to a social order and ruthlessly determined to uphold his ideal of individual self-sufficiency. Johannes Gäntschow is the extreme individualist *par excellence*. We have seen how, like his forefathers, he develops into a cold-blooded egotist who severs all ties with his fellow beings. We noted in the preceding chapter that Fallada was here certainly not indicating his admiration, in the manner of the „blood and soil" ideology, for the conception of the „natural" hero. He shows, rather, how extreme individualism develops into self-love which in turn takes the social form of complete isolationism. And the judgment Fallada passes on such an attitude is, as we have seen, quite explicit. At one point in the story Johannes Gäntschow declares: „Keine Scheu vor Gerede, nicht die Bohne Konvention, ich bin ich, und wenn es euch nicht passt, so bin ich noch lange ich. Ich, Johannes Gäntschow. GÄNTSCHOW!" [5] Here we have what Hans Fallada would refer to as a „Schrulle", one of those „Eigenbrötler, die aus eigener Gnade und eigener Machtvoll-

---

[5]   *Wir hatten mal ein Kind*, p. 163.

kommenheit nur dem eigenen Piepmatz Zucker geben", as he puts
it in the passage quoted above. Johannes Gäntschow rejects the
subordination of the individual in love and refuses to be educated
by the woman in the school of marriage. He resents the domination
of the loving and characterful woman in marriage, refuses to
permit any intrusions into his self-sufficiency and will at no cost
sacrifice part of his individuality for the sake of a happy marriage.
The result is the failure of marriage which for Fallada, as for
Gottfried Keller, was the most important trial for the individual
in the process of winning citizenship. Both Elise and Christiane
fail to turn this extreme individualist into a responsible member of
society. And so Johannes Gätschow remains completely isolated,
„eine Insel auf der Insel". He is a person who reads no newspapers
because the affairs of the world in which he lives are of no
interest to him. He is an individual who refuses to communicate
with his fellow men because for him speaking has always been
„eine ziemlich unfruchtbare Beschäftigung". Old Reese pleads
with him to realise that the individual cannot be a true self in
complete isolation from the rest of human society:

„Aber das siehst du nun ja wohl ein: jeder braucht jeden einmal..."
. . . .
„Das gibt es doch nicht, daß ein Mensch in seinem ganzen Leben
gar keinen Anhang findet . . . Und ganz allein gedeiht nicht einmal
ein Tier, und darum du auch nicht." [6]

But Gäntschow will not yield. Once again he sets up the sign
which his grandfather had erected in order to keep intruders from
his property and which reads:

> Hier wohnt Malte Gäntschow
> Kauft nichts – verkauft nichts
> und empfängt auch keine Besuche.

Johannes expels all women from his property and decides to
impose no limitations upon himself in the pursuit of his personal
objectives, in this case the restoration of his ancestral farm. This
is a man who will allow no considerations for others to hamper

[6] *Ibid.*, pp. 356–357.

him in his ruthless quest for complete self-gratification; his individualism has turned to self-love and a positive hatred of the rest of mankind.

Er würde von nun an genau das machen, was er wollte, und alle Leute und alle Gefühle gingen ihn einen Dreck an. Er wollte es ihnen zeigen, auf der Stelle!
. . . .
Er trieft vor Haß und Menschenverachtung. Er freut sich, da er sieht, daß sie alle verächtlich sind. Er genießt seine Einsamkeit. Er ist ein Schädling, er ist der Feind, er ist das Unsozialste, was sich nur denken läßt. [7]

And so Johannes Gäntschow never finds the way into human communion. His individualism has become anti-social to the extreme, and the eternal conflict between the self and the community finds no resolution. Here the individual's quest for self-assertion turns to „Menschenfeindlichkeit" which Fallada, as we have heard, believed should not be tolerated. At the end of this depressing but extremely powerful story the author refutes the ideal of individual self-sufficiency and shows how Gäntschow's egoistic drive leaves him utterly isolated with but the „rats of remorse" as his last companions: „Wir lassen Johannes Gäntschow allein, ihn, der das Leben seiner Ahnen noch einmal erlebt hat...... Noch einmal hat er zu spät entdeckt, daß er lieben konnte, und muß sich nun in den eigenen Fesseln von den Ratten der Gewissensbisse auffressen lassen." [8]

Ein Mann will hinauf gives another variation of the theme of individualistic self-assertion and the isolation of the individual. In the process of turning his great dream to „conquer Berlin" into reality, young Karl Siebrecht, too, develops into an unfeeling egotist, who becomes completely insensitive to the wants of his fellow beings. His individualism, like Gäntschow's, becomes so extreme that he does not recognise any limitations. He is determined to let no considerations for his fellow men hinder him in his desire to achieve his own personal, selfish ends. Siebrecht rejects all offers of help and is determined to tread the path to

[7] *Ibid.*, pp. 470–499.
[8] *Ibid.*, p. 546.

personal progress and success in complete solitude: „Und Überhaupt: ich will keines Menschen Angestellter sein, durch mich selbst will ich vorwärtskommen!" [9] He is a man who insists on his supreme right to follow his own inclinations and to live in accordance with his own dream. „Ein Mann muß nach seinem Traum leben, nach dem Stern, den er in sich trägt" is the precept that guides his behaviour. And so he, too, ultimately parts company with everyone, even with his wife and his best friend, Kalli Flau, who had been his partner and had helped him build up his transportation business. Siebrecht changes the name of the firm to „Siebrecht und Niemand" and looks forward to a life of solitariness, devoid of friendships, or any other human bonds: „Es war ihm, als habe er sich nun für alle Zukunft festgelegt. Niemand war sein Teilhaber, und niemand sollte je sein Teilhaber werden! Keine Verquicking mehr von Freundschaft und Firma, allein auf sich gestellt! Allein, allein."[10] Here we have the individual insisting on his „Recht sich auszuleben, ganz für sich allein etwas zu werden", as Hans Fallada puts it in the remarks quoted earlier. Karl Siebrecht's „gewissenloser Egoismus" finally alienates him from everyone. His social ascent has been achieved at the expense of such values as love and friendship and by means of the individual's complete disregard for his responsibilities as a member of society. As his old friend, von Senden, puts it to Siebrecht: „Du warst immerhin auch ein Ehrgeiziger und wolltest einen Traum verwirklichen — erinnerst du dich noch an die Eroberung von Berlin? Sehr rücksichtsvoll bist du auf diesem Wege gerade nicht mit den Gefühlen deiner Mitmenschen umgegangen — ..."[11]

In the figure of blind Siebenhaar, in *Der ungeliebte Mann*, Fallada once again depicts the individual determined to achieve self-gratification above all else. Here again he exhibits how extreme individualism turns to mere selfishness which in turn takes the social forms of complete isolationism and the domination of another life by a tyrannical ego. Soon after his marriage to Traute, Siebenhaar drops the mask he had worn in his role of the suf-

[9] *Ein Mann will hinauf*, p. 189.
[10] *Ibid.*, p. 425.
[11] *Ibid.*, p. 599.

fering and lonely individual, who bears his tragic lot with patience and dignity. He now sets to work to turn his young wife into a mere tool for the attainment of his own self-interest. As we have seen, Traute soon finds herself no better off than a slave. She becomes completely dominated by a tyrannical egotist, a man who is almost insane in his jealousy and possessiveness, who is determined to make her „zu seinem Geschöpf" and to protect his „possession" with all possible means at his disposal. And Hans Fallada comments: „Die Hüllen sind gefallen, nackt zeigt sich der Egoist, der seinen Besitz verteidigt, mit allen Mitteln." [12]

One cannot fail to read the novels we have just cited as rituals of expiation or scapegoat rituals, in which Hans Fallada castigated the „ewige alte Egoist" that he always freely admitted he was. These are works that sprang from the depths of Fallada's own experiences and in which he tried to rid himself of his vice by presenting it in a sublimated form and shaping it to some significant symbolic purpose.

In these novels, as we have seen, the individual believes his isolation to be an ideal worthy of being preserved at all costs. The individual is lonely of his own free choice; he consciously puts up a fight for his isolation; he wants to be true to himself and strives for individual self-sufficiency and demands individualistic self-fulfillment for its own sake. The lone wolf wants to be lonely and refuses to be tamed into a sense of social responsibility; he refuses to develop a communal spirit and to seek means of overcoming his isolation. And the judgment which Hans Fallada passes on this kind of isolationism has been made clear.

The novels to which we shall now turn our attention, depict, in contrast, the individual forever conscious of his isolation, but conscious of it as more of a tragic curse than a blessing. Here the individual finds himself engulfed in an isolation which is not of his own choosing, and he is constantly intent on overcoming his aloneness and finding a path that leads into an area of meaningful social activity and participation in the life of the

---

[12] *Der ungeliebte Mann*, p. 212.

community. Here, too, Hans Fallada sets forth the forces which he believed are capable of helping the individual to emerge from his isolation and indicates what might have been the ideal of human social intercourse he envisaged.

In the first chapter of this study we discussed the figure of Fallada's „little man". We noted that, as a member of the white-collar class, the acute lack of a sense of belonging and social identity constitutes one of his distinctive characteristics. We observed that Fallada's *Kleinbürger* is socially displaced and that the members of his social class are without a *Zusammenhang*, a common social and spiritual bond and a union of common purposes. We saw also how all these factors make for the atmosphere of infinite loneliness which surrounds the „little man", Pinneberg, in *Kleiner Mann – was nun?* speaks for all his brothers when he says to his wife: „Wir sitzen allein. Und die andern, die genau so sind wie wir, die sitzen auch allein." [13]

Hans Fallada's „little man", then, whether his name is Tredup, Pinneberg or Kufalt, is socially and spiritually isolated, alone and adrift in the sea of a society in which there seems to be no meaningful place for him. It is not necessary for us to add to what we have already said regarding this isolation when we discussed the novels in which Fallada depicts the plight of the *Kleinbürger*. In these works the author shows the „little man" always seeking some way out of his isolation, his „auswegloseste Einsamkeit", as Kufalt puts it at one point in *Wer einmal aus dem Blechnapf frißt*. In contrast to the isolation of such individualists as Gäntschow and Siebrecht, however, the „little man's" loneliness is not of his own making. It is, rather, felt to be a dreadful bane, and the „little man" constantly tries to establish some relationship to the rest of the human community to which he belongs. We saw in our second chapter that Hans Fallada suggests the social institution of marriage as the first means of breaking through the isolation of the individual. A healthy marriage, for Fallada, always produces children, thus iniating a process of mutuality on a wider scale than that established by the rela-

[13]   *Kleiner Mann – was nun?*, p. 293.

tionship of two people held together in the bond of matrimony. In marriage the individual is for the first time drawn out of himself and takes his first step into a human community. Here he develops a sense of social responsibility; he learns to submerge his lonely ego in a collective body and to live for the sake of the members of his family. We have heard Hans Fallada refer to the family, in *Der eiserne Gustav,* as the pillar of the state – „der Grundpfeiler vom Staat" – and to marriage, in *Der ungeliebte Mann,* as „eine Gemeinsamkeit zweier Menschen, das beseligende Gefühl: du bist nie mehr mit nichts allein auf dieser Welt". We have seen how such uncompromising individualists as Johannes Gäntschow and Karl Siebrecht fail to preserve this *Gemeinsamkeit.* Marriage, in Fallada's view, is the most important link with the social world. Real citizenship is always gained by first passing the important tests set by the school of marriage, which is seen as the very source of social order. The important part which the woman plays in this school has already been noted. Fallada's women always maintain a connection with the world, and the individual who refuses to be educated by the woman fails to find a way into society and to become one of its responsible members.

Ultimately, it is the power of human love which Hans Fallada suggests as the force which melts away the barriers that surround the individual. Love is the essential element for the establishment of the communion of two people in marriage, of the communion of more persons in the social unit of the family, and it is, ultimately, the most important factor in the communion of a large number of people in society itself. Whatever the limits of the community into which the individual is placed may be, love is the glue that sticks its members together. Love is the very marrow of society, and whenever this substance is missing, the structure of society crumbles and breaks apart into atomic pieces of isolated individuals. This, as we have noted, is the case in works such as *Bauern, Bonzen und Bomben* and *Der ungeliebte Mann,* where Fallada speaks of all the characters being isolated and unhappy because they live „in einer liebeleeren Welt", and it is, above

all, the case in *Wolf unter Wölfen* where the members of a society
are portrayed as living the lives of beasts of prey.

The title of *Wolf unter Wölfen* immediately suggests, of course,
an inorganic concept of society and constitutes, at the same time,
a harsh criticism of such a concept. Here Hans Fallada portrays
society as a mere aggregation of individuals who make up what
is essentially nothing more than a pack of lone and hungry wolves.
Each individual is as isolated as the other and each is as intent
as the other on defending his own self-interest. In the chaos of
the Inflation, in an age that is lacking any standards of value, in
which there is no more confidence in anything or anyone, each
individual member of society is forced to fight for survival in
complete isolation. Even the most organic human relationships
have been disrupted, with children facing their own parents in
a deadly antagonism:

Allein bist du, allein bin ich, allein sterben wir alle – rette sich wer
kann!

. . . .

Es ist hungrige Zeit, Wolfzeit. Die Söhne haben sich gegen die eigenen
Eltern gekehrt, das hungrige Wolfrudel fletscht gegeneinander die
Zähne – wer stark ist, lebe! Aber wer schwach ist, der sterbe! Und
er sterbe unter meinem Biß! [14]

Men who had once been close friends meet again, only to make
the painful discovery that their old ties of friendship have become
meaningless in a time in which the individual is forced to make
the struggle for survival his only consideration and in which there
is no common cause to bind people together. Thus von Prackwitz,
contemplating the solitary position into which the social and
political upheavals of the post-World War I years have thrown
not only himself but also all the others, declares: „... jeder war
für sich allein; es gab keinen Zusammenhalt, keine Gemeinsamkeit
mehr." And when he and von Studmann offer their help to their
old friend and comrade-in-arms, Wolfgang Pagel, reminding him
that they had always stood together in times of need during the
war, young Pagel answers them bitterly: „Weil ... wir damals

[14] *Wolf unter Wölfen*, I, 163, 195.

für eine Sache kämpften. Heute kämpft jeder für sich allein –
und gegen alle." [15] The united front presented by the members
of society in the face of a common enemy crumbles just as soon
as the threat has disappeared, thus underlining all the more its
tenuous nature.

All the characters in *Wolf unter Wölfen* are completely isolated.
But again, it is not of their own free choice but rather as the
result of the cruel times, the „hungrige Zeit" in which they live,
that these men and women are lonely. They are constantly searching for a way into communion with others but their longing
remains forever unsatisfied. Petra Ledig represents the very
embodiment of this tragic isolation of the individual. Forsaken
by all, even by her only loved one, she finds herself in prison
in the company of the last refuse of humanity. It is here that she
breaks out into an inner cry of utter despair at man's essential
loneliness in the world. It is a cry which, with its sorrowful over-
tones, could well stand as the very formulation of what Hans
Fallada had himself felt to be the most basic experience of his
own sad existence and which aligns him with the existentialist
thinkers and writers of our troubled age:

Ein Gefühl äußerster Verlassenheit hatte sie mit seinem Eiseshauch
angeblasen und alles in ihr erstarren lassen. Am Ende war jeder ganz
für sich allein – was die andern taten, sagten, trieben, es war nichts.
Einen einzelnen, einzigen Menschen auf sich, schwingt die Erde durch
die Ewigkeiten von Zeit und Raum ihre Bahn, immer nur einen
einzigen allein auf sich! [16]

But this enormous novel, which is the greatest plait of narrative
Hans Fallada ever twined together and which, once again,
established not only his unique inventive and imaginative faculties
but also his unrivalled technical skill in joining a great variety
of divergent plots into a unified whole, ends on a positive and
optimistic note. Man can and must eventually enter into communion with others and realise his responsibilities to the fellow
members of society. This is indicated by Wolfgang Pagel's eventual rehabilitation. And it is, once again, the power of love which

[15] *Ibid.,* p. 359.
[16] *Ibid.,* p. 438.

leads Pagel out of his solitariness and awakens him to a consciousness of his social obligations. The love of Petra finally brings about a conciliation, not only between herself and Wolfgang but also between both of them and Pagel's stubborn and possessive old mother. And so in the end we see Wolfgang Pagel, who had always believed that: „Jeder anständige Mensch fühlt sich ein wenig für seinen Mitmenschen verantwortlich", [17] on his way to assuming a civic duty. He finally carries out his long-cherished plan to become a psychiatrist and to his mother, who is once again performing her natural role, he says: „... was ich gerne sein möchte, das ist: ein wirklicher Arzt... ich habe immer gerne mit den Menschen zu tun gehabt, ich habe gerne darüber nachgedacht, wie es in ihnen aussieht, und warum sie dies und das tun. Ich bin glücklich, wenn ich ihnen helfen kann." [18]

Hans Fallada himself, incidentally, once in his life actively demonstrated how earnestly he believed that each individual should do justice to his social responsibilities when, at the urgings of the Russian occupation authorities, he assumed the civic duty of mayor of the little town of Feldberg in Mecklenburg shortly after the end of World War II. This period of public service was marked by many disillusioning experiences which repeatedly demonstrated to Fallada the inability of members of the community to act in a selfless manner for the sake of the restoration of the communal well-being. There are important statements to this effect in those parts of the semi-autobiographical novel *Der Alpdruck* that recount this phase of the author's career. There can be very little doubt that one of the factors that contributed to the nervous breakdown which terminated Fallada's career in the service of society after only four months, was the bitter realisation that he had failed in his attempt to aid in lifting the oppressive *Alpdruck* which weighed so heavily on his beloved Germany. The degree of disappointment in this book can be measured by the fact that for the first and only time in his entire work, Fallada here lets his main character voice the idea of emigration from his homeland.

[17] *Ibid.*, II, 751.
[18] *Ibid.*, 1139.

In *Der eiserne Gustav* Hans Fallada shows how the lack of love and understanding leads to the breakup of the social unit of the family. We have already observed that it is primarily the struggle between generations which brings about the dissolution of the Hackendahl family. Here our author depicts the individual asserting his freedom at the price of a struggle against parental authority which in turn results in the disruption of a human community. The individual denies his membership in the family and finds himself in isolation as a consequence. Again the individual's essential loneliness, his isolation even from those who are closest to him and with whom he is most organically connected, is made painfully clear. As old Hackendahl puts it in his simple words to his youngest son, Heinz, who has reported his brother, Erich, to the police, despite the fact that his father had pleaded with him not to betray his own brother:

Haste's also doch jesagt! Na ja, halb und halb ha' ick mir det schon so jedacht. Du kannst eben ooch nich aus deine Pelle. Ick nich und du ooch nich. Det is, wat einem so schwer injeht, det der andere ooch seine Pelle für sich apart hat. Man denkt immer: der muß doch in dieselbe Pelle stecken wie du, is doch ooch bloß Menschenpelle. Und dabei is se janz anders. [19]

The fact that the human condition is such that it is dictated by the realisation that „keiner kann aus seiner Haut", as Otto Hackendahl puts it at one point, makes the preservation of even the most organic human bonds impossible. Again we cannot help but think of the bitter alienation between father and son in Hans Fallada's own life.

Another form of the isolation of the individual is chastised by the author in *Altes Herz geht auf die Reise*. Here it is the voluntary severance of the self from the world. This is a withdrawal, however, that is unlike that of a Gäntschow or a Siebrecht in that it is not born out of a feeling of hostility but out of a mood of resignation. The individual has torn himself away from the rest of society and has retreated into a little sanctuary of his own, both outwardly and inwardly. Old Professor Gotthold Kittguss,

[19] *Der eiserner Gustav*, p. 646.

who has had „weder Weib noch Kind" in his life, has withdrawn
from the struggles of the world into a self-chosen solitude. It is
the tendency and atmosphere of the *Biedermeier* that comes to
the fore. Kittguss has been leading a monastic form of life for
many years, entombed in his dusty study where he is engaged
in obscure and rather fruitless biblical studies of the Apocalypse.
But Fallada takes the old heart on a journey and, as we saw in
the preceding chapter, exposes him to the regenerative forces of
a life spent in close harmony with nature. And here, in a simple
rural community, a new world rises up to teach the old intellectual.
He undergoes a process of rejuvenation and soon realises that
„das gemütliche, stille Gelehrtenzimmer" in which he had secluded
himself in search of some sort of satisfaction and „revelation"
had always been nothing but a grey and dark „Höhle der Eigensucht und der Unfruchtbarkeit". He becomes aware of the fruit-
lessness of the hypothetical studies which consumed so many
of his years and of the need for „ein werktätiges Christentum".
Love suddenly acquires a completely new dimension for Professor
Kittguss. Confronted with the love of the boy Philip for Rosemarie,
he suddenly becomes conscious of the social meaning and relevance of the power of love:

Er sah sie strahlend an, armer Narr, der er war, ein Zukurzgekom-
mener des Lebens – von der ersten Kindheit an. Zu kurz gekommen –
dieser arme Dorftrottel trug eine solche Liebeskraft im Herzen – :
der Professor mußte, ob es auch Sünde war, des Briefes vom Apostel
Paulus an die Korinther gedenken: „Die Liebe ... verträgt alles, sie
glaubet alles, sie hoffet alles, sie duldet alles ..." [20]

It is his good fortune that the old scholar learns to comprehend
„den rechten Lebenssinn" before it is too late. He learns that man
as a citizen of this world has not one but two dimensions of
existence, and that it amounts to nothing more than cultivating
„ein eigensüchtiges Leben" if he does justice to the one, his
spiritual or religious nature, at the expense of the other, his social
character. It is obvious that Professor Kittguss' withdrawal from
society never amounts to an aggressive and hostile shunning of
all relations with his fellow beings. Nevertheless, Hans Fallada

[20] *Altes Herz geht auf die Reise*, p. 73.

clearly feels that, no matter what form the individual's isolation takes, it always constitutes a grave threat to the proper functioning of society if the individual thereby neglects to do full justice to his social obligations.

With a brilliance of psychological insights never attained by Hans Fallada before or after, he again deals with the problem of the loneliness of the individual in the autobiographical story *Der Trinker*. This time the individual, despite his efforts, fails to find a way out from his isolation. On the very first page of the novel, Erwin Sommer admits that he suffers greatly because of his feeling of solitude and that he does not dare to reveal his plight to anyone: „Ich wollte mir um keinen Preis merken lassen, wie sehr ich unter ...meiner Vereinsamung litt." Man's loneliness here becomes the very essence of his being, filling his heart to the point where no other feelings find admittance: „... ich war grenzenlos allein mit mir und meinem Mißgeschick. Mein Herz war so übervoll davon, daß nichts anderes mehr hineinkonnte" [21] Sommer is out in the fields when he realises the extent of his terrible isolation, and the refreshing experience of his beloved nature fails so soothe his tormented soul. Finally for Erwin Sommer the excessive indulgence in drink becomes a means of escape from the pressures of his lonely existence. Being transported into a world of nothingness – „fort ins Nichts!" – dying „einen befristeten Tod" becomes preferable to having to endure the cruel experience of isolation. When in the end Sommer is expelled from society and left to conclude his sorry life amongst the „letzte Ausschuß der Menschheit", we get yet another aspect of the problem of the isolation of the individual. Here it is the forceful social isolation of the individual from the rest of society. The individual has become „gemeingefährlich" and is, consequently, ejected from the normal flow of human social intercourse. The institutional safeguarding of the individual who has become a menace to society from any relations with the rest of the world had, of course, already been depicted in *Wer einmal aus dem Blechnapf frißt*. And in many of his other novels, such as, for instance, *Bauern, Bonzen und*

[21] *Der Trinker*, p. 12.

Bomben, Wolf unter Wölfen and *Jeder stribt für sich allein,*
Fallada time and again returned to depict the individual banished
to the „Nachtseite" of existence, and exhibited man living „am
Rande des Daseins" as a member of a community of social
outcasts. In *Wer einmal aus dem Blechnapf frißt* Willi Kufalt
has become a member of a community whose confines are the
walls of a prison. In *Der Trinker* Erwin Sommer joins a community
whose confines are the walls of a mental institution. And here
Hans Fallada, once again, brings a world to view in which man
has indeed become a wolf among wolves. It is a world of the
despairing ones, the mentally ill, the perverts, the murderers, the
tortured and the torturers, and, above all, a world of the very
lonely. It is a community that has no organic ties, a community
made up of elements who are indeed the „letzte Ausschuß der
Menschheit" and dominated by the hatred and hostility of each
against all:

> Hat schon im menschlichen Leben draußen nichts dauernden Bestand,
> so kann man hier im Bau nicht fünf Minuten mit etwas Bleibendem
> rechnen. Ständig wechseln die Konstellationen, und nur das ist blei-
> bend: Der Neid und der Haß jedes gegen jeden, die tierische Feind-
> schaft aller gegen alle. Im Bunker gibt's keine Treue, keine Freund-
> schaft, nicht den primitivsten Anstand.
> "Friß, oder du wirst gefressen, Sommer!" [22]

Seldom has a writer brought the actualities of lives so widely
removed from the commonly known ones so clearly before
the eyes of the reader. Seldom have we come to experience
so intensely the feeling of bitter aloneness that dominates those
unfortunate members of the human race whose tragic lot it is to
exist, engulfed in their sorry selves, in a world that is beyond
the reaches of the saving forces of love and friendship and for
all of whom Erwin Sommer speaks when he breaks out into the
tormented cry: „Ich bin völlig allein mit mir, ich bin mir klar:
ich werde von nun an immer völlig allein mit mir sein. Ich bin
dort, wohin weder Liebe noch Freundschaft reichen. Ich bin in
der Hölle...". [23]

---

[22] *Ibid.,* p. 153.
[23] *Ibid.,* p. 131.

Our foregoing discussion of the problem of the isolation of the individual has been primarily concerned with a sociological point of view. We have regarded the individual first and foremost as a category of sociology; we have considered the position of the individual in relation to the material and the social world, to the social institution of marriage, the social unit of the family and to society itself. We have seen that Hans Fallada rejected that voluntary, egocentric isolation of the invidual in relation to the social world which takes the form of individualistic self-assertion and egoistic self-affirmation. We have noted that the majority of Fallada's characters have to endure the experience of an isolation which is not of their own choice, and that our author always stresses the need for a communal spirit. The most explicit statement of this belief is the passage we quoted from *Heute bei uns zu Haus* which does not, we believe, leave the author open to the suspicion that he was in fact paying lip service to the philosophy of the corporate state led by the Nazis. For, as we have already noted, Fallada in the same passage also expresses his strong conviction that, as far as the individual's spiritual and intellectual stature and freedom are concerned, there must be „Respekt vor Eigenart". The individuality of each person, his uniqueness and originality, must never be infringed upon or suppressed. There can be no question where Hans Fallada stands in this respect.

We shall now, finally, turn to inquire what views Fallada voiced on the ultimate religious transcendence of the individual over himself and the community. What has our author to say about the individual's desire to overcome his isolation and to emerge from his subjectivity by finding the path that leads, not into society, but into that realm where there takes place the meeting and communion with God, with a Reality that goes beyond man's social being? What has he to say about man in relation to universal obligations and religious values and about man's ultimate and supreme freedom in the religious realm? And what, finally, were Hans Fallada's views on the social relevance of the religious transcendence of the individual?

The most immediate answer to these questions is that in most of his novels Hans Fallada has very little or nothing at all to say on the question of the transcendental world and man's relation to it. Most of Fallada's characters do not experience a religious transcendence. They are, indeed, hardly aware of the fact that man is a being who does not belong to the social world alone. And this makes for an even greater intensification of their feeling of solitude. The majority of Fallada's men and women are unaware of the fact that man has a dimension which allows him to seek and find some final meaning of his life beyond the vicissitudes of the material and the social world. They have no God to speak to in their bitter solitariness. And their most prominent existential experience is the constant awareness that they will have to face the end of their lonely lives, death itself, in complete aloneness. Fallada's men and women die alone. And yet in his last great novel, which bears the title *Jeder stirbt für sich allein*, Hans Fallada repudiated the belief expressed in the title of the book and asserted that man need not die alone, and here, for the first and only time, gave some answers to the questions we have just posed.

This novel, which the author, in a supreme effort, wrote when he was in effect already a dying man, bears witness to the fact that Fallada was well aware that man is a being who belongs not to one world but to two, and that only if we regard man within this context may we do full justice to his whole stature. Otto Quangel, the main character in *Jeder stirbt für sich allein*, is a man who has always lived in isolation from his fellow beings. Never has he been concerned about the feelings or actions of other people. The only communion he has known is that with his wife. His pride has been to lead a life, engulfed in himself, in complete seclusion from the rest of the world: „Es war immer sein Stolz gewesen in diesem seinem Leben, ein Mensch ganz für sich allein zu sein, die andern nicht zu brauchen, ihnen nie lästig zu fallen..." [24] And again Hans Fallada brings a world to view in which man has become a beast of prey. It is a world in which man is lonely and threatened at all junctures by his fellow beings;

[24] *Jeder stirbt für sich allein*, p. 429.

a world of betrayed and betrayers, hunted and hunters. „Wie stehen wir da?", says the lawyer Toll to his old friend Harteisen, „Der Sohn verrät die Mutter, die Schwester den Bruder, der Freund die Freundin..." [25] And it is a world in which, above all, there is no more trust and belief in God: „An Gott konnte niemand mehr glauben; es war unmöglich, daß ein gütiger Gott solche Schande, wie sie heute auf der Welt war, zuließ...".[26]

And yet, into the midst of this cruel world Hans Fallada places human beings who have achieved that religious transcendence which raises them above the social world and which enables them to endure and to mitigate the plight of this earthly existence. It is these characters who point the way to another path that leads man out from his loneliness and on which he may reach his ultimate freedom over the material world.

In the figure of Ulrich Heffke, Otto Quangel's pious brother-in-law, Hans Fallada rebukes that form of piety which, by refusing to recognise man's social responsibilities and abandoning everything earthly, becomes the highest form of egoism. Heffke's position is somewhat similar to that of Professor Kittguss prior to the journey that opened his eyes to the worthwhile realities of life. Heffke is a man who has surmounted and transcended himself by simply transporting himself into a realm of mystic otherworldliness in which the singing of religious hymns becomes his only occupation. He is the religious fanatic who assumes no civic duty and rightly deserves Quangel's bitter reproach: „Weil die an den Himmel glauben, wollen sie auf der Erde nichts ändern. Immer nur kriechen und sich drücken!" [27] But there are other men in this book who have grasped the true meaning of the religious transcendence of the individual. Such is the judge, Fromm, such is the musician, Dr. Reichhardt, and such, above all, is the prison-parson, Pastor Lorenz. Here Fallada has portrayed men who, while appealing to a higher authority than society's approval of their actions, do not thereby emancipate themselves from their social responsibilities. Here are men who

25   *Ibid.*, p. 159.
26   *Ibid.*, p. 331.
7   *Ibid.*, p. 331.

live according to their ideals and innermost beliefs and who become the most effective opponents of the tyrannical rule because, while obeying the commandment to love God above everything else, they do not forget that other commandment which bids man love his neighbour as himself.

Fromm is a man „der nur der Gerechtigkeit gehorcht". He has never permitted any other consideration to determine his actions, and he remains true to his ideal even at a time when it could mean his own destruction. Unmindful of the consequences, he helps his fellow beings whenever they are in need because, as he puts it to Frau Rosenthal, the old Jewess whom he has offered a refuge in his home: „Ich habe eine Herrin, der ich zu gehorchen habe, sie regiert mich, Sie, die Welt, selbst die Welt jetzt draußen, und diese Herrin ist die Gerechtigkeit. An sie habe ich immer geglaubt, glaube ich heute noch, die Gerechtigkeit habe ich allein zur Richtschnur meines Handelns gemacht." [28] Here is a man who has made a higher value than any earthly decree the standard of his actions. Throughout his life he has stood alone before the throne of Justice. He has transcended the limited social world, but he has not thereby abstracted his consciousness from the world in which he lives.

The figure of the prison-clergyman, Pastor Friedrich Lorenz, is Fallada's only interpretation of a true Christian. Lorenz is a man who practices the spirit of Christianity, whose religious transcendence has at the same time become his highest form of social realisation. Stricken with a deadly lung-ailment, this mild yet determined man trudges the corridors of the prison for endless miles, bringing comfort and peace to the minds of the despairing and lonely ones and disclosing to them a new universe wherein they may find a final deliverance from their plight. He becomes Trudel Hergesell's guide into a new world of hope and joy, bringing her the message of the meaning of the coming of Christ: „. . .sie solle doch erfahren, wie einer auf dieser Erde gelebt habe, so daß seine Spur noch nach fast zweitausend Jahren unvergänglich strahle, ewiges Abbild dessen, daß die Liebe stärker sei

[28] *Ibid.*, p. 78.

als der Haß".[29] And slowly this forlorn little woman, who, we are told, had been „religionslos" throughout her life, begins to comprehend. In the company of the parson, she experiences a deep sense of joy and peace:

Trudel Hergesell hatte sich zuerst gegen eine solche Lehre aufgelehnt. Sie kam ihr gar zu weichlich vor. So war es nicht Jesus Christus, der ihr Herz empfänglich machte, sondern sein Pastor Friedrich Lorenz. Wenn sie diesen Mann betrachtete, dessen schwere Krankheit niemand übersehen konnte, wenn sie erlebte, daß er an ihren Sorgen teilhatte, als seien es seine eigenen, daß er nie an sich selbst dachte,... so empfand sie etwas wie Glück, einen tiefen Frieden, der von diesem Mann ausging, der nicht hassen, sondern nur lieben wollte, auch noch den schlechtesten Menschen lieben. [30]

Here Hans Fallada makes it clear that it is the example given in devoted service to his fellow human beings that endows a Christian's religious convictions with true meaning. In other words, it is the social relevance of our spiritual existence that matters.

Otto Quangel is also given a companion who awakens him to an awareness of that other dimension of human existence. It is in the prison-cell, while awaiting his execution, that Quangel meets the kindly conductor, Dr. Reichardt, who is able to lead him out of his isolation and who points him the way to a fuller experience of life. Dr. Reichhardt is a man who has attained to that final height of freedom where he is able to comprehend the true meaning of life and from which he can defy any and all treacherous earthly forces. His loving-kindness knows of no distinctions between his fellow creatures. When Quangel reproaches him for being too kindly and understanding, even to those who hate and despise him, Reichardt answers him: „Wollen wir denn werden wie die andern, Quangel? Die glauben doch, daß sie uns mit Schlägen zu ihren Ansichten bekehren können! Aber wir glauben nicht an die Herrschaft der Gewalt. Wir glauben an Güte, Liebe, Gerechtigkeit." [31] And furthermore he tells

[29] *Ibid.*, p. 466.
[30] *Ibid.*, pp. 466–467.
[31] *Ibid.*, p. 454.

Quangel that the individual cannot fulfill his life in isolation but only in responsible relations with others, and that man must ultimately realise himself in the lives of his fellow-men: „Wir leben nicht für uns, sondern für die andern. Was wir aus uns machen, machen wir nicht für uns aus uns, sondern nur für die andern...".[32] It is in the company of this loving and considerate man that Otto Quangel, a man „der sich nie was aus den Menschen gemacht hat", finally undergoes a profound spiritual rebirth. He begins to realise the futility of his own life, spent in a self-chosen isolation, in which he had at all times refused to enter into communion with others: „...manchmal kamen ihm Zweifel, ob er denn sein eigenes Leben wohl auf die richtige Art geführt hätte, getrennt von allen andern, ein Leben selbstgewollter Vereinzelung... Ja, es war kein Zweifel: über die Fünfzig hinaus, gewiß eines nahen Todes, wandelte sich Quangel noch."[33]

And so at the end of his life, it is a totally changed Otto Quangel who walks, unbroken in spirit, to the place of his execution. It is a man who has achieved an awareness of his full stature, of the ultimate freedom of the individual beyond the confines of the mundane world. Reichardt has taught him to recognise that his life will find its ultimate fulfillment beyond his earthly existence; he has, above all, taught him a broader ideal of human brotherhood than any which may be realised in this world, a brotherhood that assures us that even in death we need not be alone: „So haben wir alle einzeln handeln müssen, und einzeln sind wir gefangen, und jeder wird für sich allein sterben müssen. Aber darum sind wir doch nicht allein, Quangel, darum sterben wir doch nicht umsonst." [34] In this novel, which Johannes R. Becher in the article mentioned earlier has rightly termed Hans Fallada's „Vermächtnis", we learn how desperately and with what earnestness Fallada struggled to find some religious solutions to the problems of his terribly lonely and tormented existence. Did he succeed, even in a small measure, in his own life? The evidence

---

[32] *Ibid.*, p. 456.
[33] *Ibid.*, p. 456.
[34] *Ibid.*, p. 458.

seems to suggest that he failed. Shortly before his death, he confessed to Felix Riemkasten in these bitter words:

Manchmal habe ich mich nach religiösen Auswegen gesehnt, aber da mir jeder Sinn und jedes Bedürfnis fehlt, so ist es nie etwas geworden. Ich bin wahrhaftig schlimmer als ein Heide, ich glaube einfach gar nischt... Mit dem ganzen Treiben der Berliner Welt habe ich kaum noch etwas zu schaffen. Ich wohne hier weit ab vom Getriebe der Welt... Ohne Ausweis kommt keiner zu mir. Ich kann den ganzen Tag arbeiten und brauche niemanden zu sehen... Ich bin der einzige alte Mann im Haus... Ich bin der ganzen Sache so müde, einfach müde...[35]

And then Hans Fallada, the „zeitloser Zauberer", as Becher has called him, died. He died in that „graue Vereinsamung" in which he had been engulfed throughout his life. Hans Fallada, wasted through the excessive use of alcohol and drugs to a mere shadow of his former self, died alone.[36] We are left with his novels which bear on their pages the marks of the author's lonely and tragic existence and show his constant preoccupation with the existential problem of the essential loneliness of man faced with dread, failure and death. And yet these books are also always joyous hymns to life. They can in a very real sense be called „Daseinsgläubig". Hans Fallada never fails to stress the need for man to put up with the horrors of existence, to live on, inspite of everything. „Weiterleben!" is an admonition frequently heard throughout all of his works. That in this human life there may yet be joy, a joy that transcends our woe and makes it worth our while to live on, is Hans Fallada's ultimate faith. All his novels, indeed, ultimately end with a heroic „Yea" to life; they are in fact dedicated to life, „dem unbezwinglichen, immer von neuem über Schmach und Tränen, über Elend und Tod triumphierenden Leben".[37]

---

[35] Felix Riemkasten, „Nachwort" to: *Hoppelpoppel – wo bist du?.* Kindergeschichten, von Hans Fallada (Stuttgart, Reclam-Verlag, 1955), pp. 75–76.
[36] For a moving account of the tragic last period of Fallada's life, see: Jürgen Manthey, *op. cit.,* pp. 150ff.
[37] *Jeder stirbt für sich allein,* p. 536.

V

HANS FALLADA'S LEGACY

In closing an attempt must be made to assess Hans Fallada's achievements and his peculiar position in German literature of the twentieth century. One fact no one would dispute about our author is his continuing popularity. This popularity is, of course, no longer at its *Kleiner Mann – was nun?* peak; but it is nevertheless still very much in evidence. The most immediate question which crops up in this connection is whether a writer of such popular talent can also be a true artist. Has Hans Fallada, in other words, succeeded in bridging the gap between mere entertainment and art, *Unterhaltung* and *Kunst?* We feel that he has, and we believe, furthermore, that *Unterhaltung* and *Kunst* are not necessarily mutually exclusive. There are definite and plausible reasons why Hans Fallada's books make good and popular reading; but these are not reasons that could be cited in support of a contention that his works are not true art. The fact that the idyllic element often triumphs in Fallada's works in doubtless one important factor which accounts for his popularity. But in this respect Hans Fallada stands in a highly respectable German literary tradition which includes such great nineteenth century novelists as Wilhelm Raabe and Adalbert Stifter. Another reason for Fallada's lasting success with the readers simply lies in the fact that he is an extremely skillful storyteller. At a time when so many modern novelists are experimenting with far-out techniques and we are witnessing a rapid decline in the true and original epic art of good storytelling, when we see modern novels invading such foreign fields as those of philosophy, psychology, history and economics, to name just a few, Hans

Fallada's works represent a rebirth and reassertion of narrative vigour in modern German literature. If much has been said about the death of the story in the arid field of contemporary fiction, we can take heart from the works of Hans Fallada; for here, once again, we are surrounded by that atmosphere of tangibility which has always been the hallmark of great epic writing. Hans Fallada stands out as one of the liveliest epic talents in modern German literature.

It would be wrong, however, to assume that Fallada was nothing more than a mere realistic storyteller. In „Wie ich Schriftsteller wurde" he states most emphatically that he never considered himself to be a naturalist simply reproducing reality as it is but that he always strove to be an artist who depicted *Natur* „wie sie sich in mir ansammelt in der Auswahl, in der sie sich in mir ansammelt, in der Veränderung, die sie in mir erfährt".[1] Works such as *Bauern, Bonzen und Bomben, Wer einmal aus dem Blechnapf trißt, Wolf unter Wölfen, Wir hatten mal ein Kind, Kleiner Mann — was nun?* and *Jeder stirbt für sich allein* show our author as an artist who always lets his „realistic" style be guided by a principle of artistic transformation and careful selection. There is no neglect of art for the sake of truth in Fallada's novels. There is always thoughtful composition; there is the expert use of details to achieve the most impressive effect; there is the unique handling of the dialogue as a means not only of characterisation but also of narrative progression; there is sometimes the clever employment of the devices of modern film-making; and there is, above all, always one of the most vivid and plastic character drawing in German literature of the twentieth century.

The foregoing comments on Hans Fallada's narrative techniques are intended as nothing more than a brief summing up of the chief characteristics of his style. We purposely refrained from discussing this subject in this study, since, as mentioned earlier, we feel there is no need to elaborate on Theodor Lemmer's findings in his

---

1   „Wie ich Schriftsteller wurde", contained in: Hans Fallada, *Gesammelte Erzählungen* (Reinbek bei Hamburg, Rowohlt Verlag, 1967), p. 310.

dissertation on Fallada. We recommend Lemmer's work to those particularly interested in this aspect of Fallada's writings.

Some might argue that as an artist Fallada was not what can be termed a „thinker". Again this might very well constitute a reason for his popularity. In the introduction of an American college edition of Fallada's novel *Zwei zarte Lämmchen – weiß wie Schnee* the book is referred to as being „distinguished by a rare quality of sophisticated simplicity".[2] This statement applies equally as well to most of Hans Fallada's other novels. Unhampered by *Bildung* and complicated introspection of any sort, Fallada nevertheless saw and revealed candidly some of the basic issues of our modern social life and of human existence in general. His books are rarely interrupted for explicit analysis or reflection, and yet they reveal a deep psychological, social and even philosophical insight; an insight born of the author's own rich experience and of his profound understanding of the condition of modern man. It was the kind of insight, above all, that could be communicated to a large segment of the reading public. Hans Fallada was in fact able to register the whole scale of emotions and values by which the „average" human being lives.

Fallada's pet, however, always remained the „little man", the German *Kleinbürger*. Here again our author occupies a unique position in modern German literature. It is to him, more than to any other German writer of the period between the two World Wars, that credit must be given for having undertaken and fulfilled the important task of shedding considerable light on the lot of the German *Kleinbürgertum* during that complicated and dislocated era of modern German history. The apolitical figure of the displaced petit-bourgeois, who is dependent on and threatened by life in the modern city and the fluctuations of modern industrialism and who fails to assert himself against an uncomprehending bourgeois society, especially in the varying social, economic and political conditions of post-World War I Germany, stands at the very centre of our author's most important novels.

[2] *Zwei zarte Lämmchen – weiß wie Schnee*, ed. Hanna Hafkesbrink (Boston, Houghton Mifflin Company, The Riverside Press, Cambridge, Mass., 1958), p. V.

It is a grievous omission that it has not as yet been fully recognised that Hans Fallada, as *the* author of the German *Kleinbürgertum,* fills an important void in German literature.

It has become evident throughout our investigation that Hans Fallada is not a „social" writer in the ordinary sense of that term. If we were to consider him as such, a great many of his novels, among them some of his best, would obviously have to be ignored in a discussion of his works. Fallada's relationship to his characters is not that of a rational critical observer but rather one of deep emotional involvement. It is always quite apparent that an impassioned humanistic concern predominates in Fallada's social criticism. While exhibiting and examining critically the peculiar social status of his „little man", our author always allows for the ultimate importance of the individual. His social thinking and criticism must, then, be viewed in an essentially private yet nevertheless universal context. Even though in works such as *Bauern, Bonzen und Bomben, Wolf unter Wölfen,* and *Der eiserne Gustav* we do have some pointed political criticism directed at the Weimar Republic, Fallada's main concern was never with ephemeral political and collective issues and temporary social conditions but, rather, with certain fundamental and timeless human problems and conflicts and with the state of mind engendered in the victims of whatever conditions may prevail at a certain time in society. Many of Fallada's „little men" are indeed „victims of society", but they are never exploited as such by the author. Their lot is never portrayed as being solely the result of social and economic factors. More often than not it is the individual's own shortcomings that prove to be a much more dangerous menace to human happiness. It is the tragedy of the individual rather than the forces that shape the individual's destiny that moves us most in Fallada's works. Hans Fallada, then, never considered man's existential predicament as a mere social problem. As a critic of social life he was certainly not a reformer. His conclusions are never „revolutionary" but they nevertheless always have relevance to a level of experience that is the common property of humanity. His books are social and historical documentaries, but at the same time they are a great

deal more than mere *Zeitdokumente*. It is clear that Hans Fallada
had no fixed ideas or programs for the correction of any prevalent
social wrongs, and that he was wary of all political doctrines that
claim to be panaceas. It is, however, equally clear that his
realistic presentation of the plain truth points indirectly in the
direction of a moral lesson and demonstrates, above all, the need
for a sympathetic attitude towards the sufferings of the unfortunate members of our society. Compassion, ultimately, is Hans
Fallada's most persistent trait.

In Fallada's work an escape from the social, economic and
political pressures of our dislocated modern age always lies in a
retreat into man's private life. This represents an important
recollection and reappraisal of certain fundamental human bonds
and values. It is in this connection that the theme of marriage
assumes its significance in Fallada's work. For Hans Fallada a
healthy marriage is the very source of human tranquility and
social order. The woman plays the decisive role in the marital
relationship; she is the most important educative force; she
guards society's most precious values and maintains a healthy
connection with the social world. Fallada sees the bond of marriage
as the most important means of integrating the individual into
society. For the socially displaced „little man" marriage sastisfies
his need for contacts and helps him to regain some sense of
personal and social identity. Ultimately Hans Fallada sees man's
salvation in a selfless surrender to the all-embracing power of
human love.

In an age dominated by numerous pressures and in times of
utter disillusionment, characterised by social and economic disintegration, Hans Fallada was clearly aware of yet another genuine
modern need. It is the need for certain incorruptible and eternal
principles, a need which is fulfilled by a recollection of man's
ties to his elemental sources and of his position as an integral
part of nature. Fallada was very conscious of the disintegrating
influences of industrialism and highly critical of a culture based
on the philosophy of materialism. And he clearly recognised and
stressed the therapeutic value for modern social life of a pattern
of life which, in its simplicity, allows for a fullness of living in its

essential and basic aspects and permits an immediacy of awareness of certain immutable values. Fallada himself became rustic and drew consolation and strength from his close contact with nature. But our author's criticism of modern industrialised social life remains equitable and blended throughout. In Hans Fallada we have no simple „return to nature". He stands, rather, in the tradition of the great and genuine German regionalists who always wrote close to nature and the land. Fallada was well aware of the fact that the mere reversal to simple agrarian forms of social life cannot effectively meet the evils and challenges of our modern age. While recognising nature and the soil as man's ultimate remaining security, Hans Fallada stresses man's need to adjust to modern society and to realise the value of techno-logical progress and cultural living. Fallada's rural talisman, while it does at times serve as an effective corrective, never assumes the qualities of a magical device capable of meeting all problems of modernism and is always ultimately conditioned by doubt as to its usefulness.

One of the basic problems of human existence which for Hans Fallada was more than a mere social issue but constituted his most persistent existential experience, was the acute awareness of man's essential loneliness in the world. Man's social and spiritual isolation ultimately stands out as the central theme of his work. Here Hans Fallada reveals himself as a deeply tragic writer. His whole work bears witness to the fact that he was profoundly critical of isolation, in whatever form it may manifest itself. His conviction is that the individual cannot be a true self in isolation. Fallada opposes individualistic self-assertion, deplores the atomisation of contemporary society and insists that man, while preserving his individuality and spiritual freedom, must do justice to his communal function and stature and realise himself in the lives of others. The need to bridge the loneliness of the individual by communal immersion is continuously stressed by the author. Even man's religious transcendence must ultimately become his highest form of social realisation if it is to find moral justification. Hans Fallada's ideal of human social intercourse seems to have been an organic community in which the life of the individual acquires meaning only as he participates in the communal whole. It is a community which, as is evident from our earlier quotations, he always refers to as a *Gemeinschaft* rather than a *Gesellschaft*, and only in one instance is the latter term used to denote society.

The foregoing study has been an attempt to do some justice to Hans Fallada's work in its voluminous entirety. It is a work which is immensely varied. Hans Fallada can be brutally realistic; he can mix realism and grotesque irony in the manner of a Dickens; he can be satirical; he can be boisterously humorous; he can be tenderly romantic; he can be strictly objective; he can be deeply emotional; he can also transport the reader into the world of the fairy tale. If we add to this diversity of artistic expression the fact that the author's true self was cruelly muffled and his poetic expression distorted during those years that he wrote under the shadow of Fascism, then it becomes all too apparent that his achievements are not at all easily summarised. It might seem little enough to say that when we ask ourselves what constitutes Fallada's legacy we have to think of such a unique figure as Lämmchen in *Kleiner Mann – was nun?*. Here, as in many other characters, Hans Fallada was able to release profound emotional forces that will surely endure the test of time. Perhaps, then, his consummate skill in human portraiture consti-tutes Hans Fallada's real greatness and his lasting achievement.

SELECTED BIBLIOGRAPHY

WORKS BY HANS FALLADA

Der junge Goedeschal (Berlin, 1920).
Anton und Gerda (Berlin, 1923).
Bauern, Bonzen und Bomben (Berlin, 1931).
Kleiner Mann – was nun? (Berlin, 1932).
Wer einmal aus dem Blechnapf frißt (Berlin, 1934).
Wir hatten mal ein Kind (Berlin, 1934).
Märchen vom Stadtschreiber, der aufs Land flog (Berlin, 1935).
Altes Herz geht auf die Reise (Berlin, 1936).
Hoppelpoppel – wo bist du? (Leipzig, 1936).
Wolf unter Wölfen (Berlin, 1937).
Der eiserne Gustav (Berlin, 1938).
Geschichten aus der Murkelei (Berlin, 1938).
Kleiner Mann – großer Mann, alles vertauscht (Stuttgart, 1939).
Süszmilch spricht (Aalen, 1939).
Der ungeliebte Mann (Stuttgart, 1940).
Das Abenteuer des Werner Quabs (Leipzig, 1941).
Damals bei uns daheim: Erlebtes, Erfahrenes und Erfundenes (Stuttgart, 1942).
Heute bei uns zu Haus: Ein anderes Buch. Erfahrenes und Erfundenes (Stuttgart, 1943).
Der Alpdruck (Berlin, 1947).
Jeder stirbt für sich allein (Berlin, 1947).
Der Trinker (Hamburg, 1950).
Ein Mann will hinauf. Die Frauen und der Träumer (München and Konstanz, 1953).
Zwei zarte Lämmchen – weiß wie Schnee (Hannover, 1953).
Die Stunde, eh' du schlafen gehst (München, 1954).
Junger Herr – ganz groß (Berlin and Frankfurt/M., 1965).
Gesammelte Erzählungen (Reinbek bei Hamburg, 1967).

SECONDARY SOURCES

Becher, Johannes R., „Was nun? Zu Falladas Tod", *Aufbau*, Jahrgang 3 (1947), Heft 2, 95–99.

Berendsohn, Walter A., *Die Humanistische Front*, Erster Teil (Zürich, 1946), pp. 34–39.

Bergholz, Harry, „Hans Fallada's Breakthrough", *German Quarterly*, 29 (1956), 19–24.

Desbarats, Jean, *Die deutsche Gesellschaft in den Romanen Hans Falladas* (diss. Faculté de Lettres de Toulouse, 1955).

Dodd, Martha, *Through Embassy Eyes* (New York, 1939).

Heinrichs, Charlotte. „Wirklichkeit und Wirksamkeit des Dichters Hans Fallada", *Berliner Hefte*, II (1947), Heft 4, 234–250.

Korn, Karl, „Moira und Schuld. Ein Bericht über neue Romane", *Die Neue Rundschau*, II (1938), 603–616.

Lange, J. M. and Geerds, H. J., „Hans Fallada". In: *Schrifsteller der Gegenwart*. VI (Berlin, 1961), pp. 77–114.

Lemmer, Theodor, *Hans Fallada. Eine Monographie* (diss. Freiburg in der Schweiz, 1961).

Lukacs, Georg, *Deutsche Literatur im Zeitalter des Imperialismus* (Berlin, 1950), pp. 711–716.

Manthey, Jürgen, *Hans Fallada. In Selbstzeugnissen und Bilddokumenten* (Reinbek bei Hamburg, 1963).

Römer, Ruth, „Dichter des Kleinbürgerlichen Verfalls. Vor zehn Jahren starb Hans Fallada", *Neue Deutsche Literatur*, V (1957), Heft 2, 120–131.

Schroeder, Max, „Hans Fallada. Zum Erscheinen seines nachgelassenen Romans „Der Trinker"", *Neue Deutsche Literatur*, Jahrgang 1 (December 1953), Heft 12, 124–130.

Slochower, Harry, „Hauptmann and Fallada: Uncoordinated Writers of Nazi Germany", *Accent*, III (1942), 18–25.

Spiero, Heinrich, *Geschichte des deutschen Romans* (Berlin, 1950).

Ter-Nedden, Eberhard, „Ein Wort über Fallada", *Bücherkunde*, Nr. 11 (1941), 326–331.

Tucholsky, Kurt, *Gesammelte Werke. III* (Reinbek bei Hamburg, 1960), pp. 820–826.

V. W., „Zum... Tode Hans Falladas", *National-Zeitung* (Basel, Nr. 67, 1947), 2.

Wyk, H. A., „Hans Fallada", *The Living Age*, CCCXLIV (1933), 328–332.

Zuckmayer, Carl, „Ein Buch (Fallada: „Kleiner Mann – was nun?"), *Die Literatur*, 35 (1932/33), 100.

INDEX OF NAMES AND TITLES

Balzac, Honoré de, 8
Becher, Johannes R., 36, 90, 111, 112

Dickens, Charles, 119
Dodd, Martha, 70–71
Through Embassy Eyes, 70

Fallada, Hans
Works:
Altes Herz geht auf die Reise, 79-82, 102-04
Anton und Gerda, 20
Bauern, Bonzen und Bomben, 9, 20-22, 23, 24, 26, 31, 33, 52, 53, 71-74, 98, 104, 105, 114, 116
Der Alpdruck, 35, 40, 61, 88, 101
Der eiserne Gustav, 28-30, 31, 57-60, 98, 102, 116
Der junge Goedeschal, 20
Der Trinker, 26-28, 46-49, 62, 104-105
Der ungeliebte Mann, 44-46, 95-96, 98
Ein Mann will hinauf, 43-44, 61, 83, 94-95
Geschichten aus der Murkelei, 86
Gesammelte Erzählungen, 7, 31, 86, 114
Heute bei uns zu Haus, 14, 25, 28, 38, 40, 48, 49, 66, 67-71, 88-91, 106
Hoppelpoppel - wo bist du?, 86
Jeder stirbt für sich allein, 35-
36, 58, 62, 82, 83, 105, 107-112, 114
Junger Herr - ganz groß, 57-58
Kleiner Mann - großer Mann, alles vertauscht, 31-34, 55-56, 79, 86
Kleiner Mann - was nun?, 13-20, 22, 23, 31, 32, 33, 49-52, 66, 79, 97, 113, 114, 119
Märchen vom Stadtschreiber, der aufs Land flog, 30, 35, 60-61, 63, 77-79
Wer einmal aus dem Blechnapf frißt, 22-25, 53-54, 84-85, 97, 104, 105, 114
Wir hatten mal ein Kind, 35, 41-43, 49, 74-75, 83, 92-94, 114
Wolf unter Wölfen, 31, 34, 35, 37, 54-55, 75-77, 99-101, 105, 114, 116
Zwei zarte Lämmchen - weiß wie Schnee, 63, 115
Fontane, Theodor, 25

Grimm, Jakob and Wilhelm, 28
Grimmelshausen, J. J. Chr. v., 8

Hauptmann, Gerhart, 8
Hoffmann, E. T. A., 60

Kafka, Franz
Die Verwandlung, 60
Keller, Gottfried, 93
Kleist, Heinrich von, 15, 54
Kracauer, Siegfried, 20

Lawrence, D. H., 28
Lemmer, Theodor, 10, 114, 115

Mann, Thomas
  Buddenbrooks, 29
Manthey, Jürgen, 8, 10, 20, 22,
  40, 62, 112

Raabe, Wilhelm, 113
Riemkasten, Felix, 112
Römer, Ruth, 24

Schiller, Friedrich von, 84
Slochower, Harry, 30, 35, 60, 65
Spiero, Heinrich, 25
Stifter, Adalbert, 113

Tucholsky, Kurt, 9
Tügel, Peter W., 29

Wyk, H. A., 39, 40, 60, 66

Zola, Emile, 8
Zuckmayer, Carl, 24, 52

STUDIES IN GERMAN LITERATURE

1. Lloyd Warren Wedberg: *The Theme of Loneliness in Theodor Storm's Novellen.* 1964. 166 pp.   f. 19.—

2. Werner Hoffmeister: *Studien zur erlebten Rede bei Thomas Mann und Robert Musil.* 1965. 173 pp. f. 24.—

4. Valters Nollendorfs: *Der Streit um den Urfaust.* 1967. 304 pp.   f. 40.—

5. Jeffrey L. Sammons: *The Nachtwachen von Bonaventura. A structural Interpretation.* 1965. 128 pp. Cloth. f. 20.—

6. William Samelson: *Gerhart Hermann Mostar: A Critical Profile.* 1966. 274 pp. Cloth.   f. 34.—

7. Roger L. Cole: *The Ethical Foundations of Rudolf Bindings' "Gentleman"-Concept.* 1966. 166 pp. f. 21.50

8. Michael M. Metzger: *Lessing and the Language of Comedy.* 1966. 248 pp. Cloth.   f. 30.—

9. Josef Thanner: *Die Stilistik Theodor Fontanes: Untersuchungen zur Erhellung des Begriffes "Realismus" in der Literatur.* 1967. 160 pp.   f. 22.—

10. Albert R. Schmitt: *Herder und Amerika.* 1967. 186 pp. f. 28.—

11. Gerhardt Edward Steinke: *The Life and Work of Hugo Ball, Founder of Dadaism.* 1967. 243 pp.   f. 26.—

12. Roger A. Nicholls: *The Dramas of Christian Dietrich Grabbe.* 1969. 268 pp.   f. 39.—

MOUTON · PUBLISHERS · THE HAGUE